The
Stoic Leader

The
Stoic Leader

Guiding Principles for Success in 12 Leadership Roles

F. Zeth Lent

For E.

Table of Contents

Introduction

"We suffer more in imagination than we do in reality"

Seneca

*I*n 2019, it was reported that 970 million people in the world were suffering with a mental disorder. It means that one person out of every 8 people was going through a psychological tragedy. Out of all of these surveys, depression and anxiety were the most commonly diagnosed mental health disorders and no common denominator was found which could be the cause of these illnesses.

While these are the people who decided to speak up and seek medical help for their problems, there are several others who choose to suffer silently to the commands of their brain. The 970 million people were only the ones who were reported their suffrage to the medical facilities. However, in reality no one knows how many people are troubled by the endless chatter of their mind.

Some people can easily rub it off by ignoring the loop of negative commentary in their minds as they consider it harmless but there are others who cannot. It is estimated that 60% of the people who commit suicide are going through major depressive episodes. Troubles such as depression, anxiety, insomnia etc., can surely be caused by our genetics. However, in most cases it is due to stress.

When a person experiences something new they feel like they have little control over a situation or something new or unexpected threatens their sense of self, they get stressed. So basically, stress is our body's reaction to dealing with external factors which are not in our control and it is also the root cause of most of the silent sufferers of the mental disorders.

Now the question arises, what can we do to mitigate such uncontrollable problems from our lives?

In a time when mental issues have taken shape of an epidemic, this is a high time to implement the teachings of the Athens into our life. It was reported that the surge in the mental illnesses in recent times could be due to the use of social media, the impact of austerity, increased income inequality, increased academic pressure in young people and so long and so forth. The only common denominator between all of these causes is that there are several external factors which are at play. These are all the factors on which a person can get any control over, which is where Stoicism comes in.

Stoicism originated in early 3rd-century BC in ancient Greece and Rome. It is a way of living that enhances good feelings, decreases unpleasant emotions, and aids people in developing their moral qualities. Stoicism offers an outline for a good life at every time, in any circumstance, and at any degree of development that a person goes through. It serves as a helpful reminder of what matters most in life and offers doable methods for obtaining more of what is worthwhile.

Stoicism was purposefully designed to be practical and helpful. It's not necessary to spend hours a day in meditation or acquire a completely new philosophical vocabulary in order to practice stoicism. Rather, it provides a quick, helpful, and realistic means of achieving peace and enhancing one's personal virtues.

In today's fast-paced world, where challenges often arise unexpectedly, a resurgence of Stoicism is evident among politicians, sportsmen, and business leaders. This ancient philosophy, rooted in practical wisdom and self-mastery, provides invaluable tools for navigating the complexities of leadership in any field.

Stoicism equips leaders with the mental strength to face adversity head-on. In politics, where decisions impact entire communities, or in the competitive arena of sports, where victory and defeat hang in the balance, this resilience is important. Business leaders, too, grapple with ever-changing markets and unforeseen challenges. Stoicism teaches them to endure, adapt, and emerge stronger from setbacks.

In the heat of the moment, decisions must be made swiftly and with clarity. All influential leaders alike benefit from the Stoic emphasis on rational thinking. This allows them to weigh options objectively, free from impulsive reactions. A Stoic leader considers the greater good and acts with a clear vision, making choices that stand the test of time.

The Stoic commitment to justice and fairness holds profound relevance in the realms of politics, sports, and business. Politicians guided by Stoicism prioritize the well-being of their constituents above personal gain. Sportsmen compete with honor and integrity, respecting both their teammates and opponents.

Business leaders make ethical choices, understanding that long-term success is built on a foundation of trust and transparency.

Leadership hinges on the ability to communicate and inspire. Stoicism emphasizes the power of words and actions. Politicians who communicate with clarity and empathy garner trust and support. Sportsmen who lead by example on and off the field inspire their teammates. In the boardroom, business leaders who communicate a clear vision motivate their teams towards shared goals.

Stoicism encourages leaders to balance empathy with assertiveness. This equilibrium is essential for effective leadership. Politicians must be compassionate advocates for their constituents, while also making tough decisions for the greater good. Sportsmen lead by supporting their teammates, yet they must also take charge in critical moments. Business leaders must strike a balance between understanding their employees' needs and driving the organization forward.

Stoicism challenges leaders to consider the lasting impact of their actions. This is especially pertinent for politicians, sportsmen, and business leaders, as their decisions reverberate through society. A Stoic leader aims to leave a legacy of integrity, inspiring others to follow in their footsteps. They understand that true leadership extends beyond personal success, shaping a better future for all.

In the resurgence of Stoicism among politicians, sportsmen, and business leaders, we witness a return to the foundational principles of effective leadership. Through resilience, ethical conduct, clear communication, and a legacy of impact, Stoicism equips leaders to navigate the complexities of their roles with wisdom and integrity. As they draw on the timeless wisdom of this philosophy, they pave the way for a new era of purposeful, impactful leadership.

In the ever-evolving landscape of leadership, the principles of Stoicism stand as a timeless beacon, offering steadfast guidance in the face of uncertainty and change. For those already acquainted with the fundamental tenets of Stoicism, this book is not a rehashing of introductory concepts. It is a blueprint, a manual crafted for leaders who seek not only to understand, but to wield the power of Stoicism in their everyday roles.

At the core of Stoic leadership lies a code, unwavering and unyielding. It is a code defined by wisdom, the ability to discern what is within our control and what lies beyond. It is rooted in courage, the strength to face adversity with equanimity. It embodies justice, an unwavering commitment to fairness and ethical conduct. And it is tempered by wisdom, the art of moderation and self-mastery. These principles form the foundation upon which Stoic leaders build their legacy.

Understanding the essence of Stoicism is but the first step. The true mastery lies in its application. Through real-life Situations and battle-tested tactics, this book bridges the gap between theory and practice. It provides a roadmap for leaders to navigate the intricate terrain of influence, whether in the boardroom, the community, or the intimate sphere of one's own home.

Leadership is not a static endeavor—it demands adaptability, versatility, and a keen understanding of the tools at one's disposal. From principled decision-making to effective communication, from conflict resolution to fostering a culture of growth, this section arms you with a comprehensive arsenal of strategies, honed in the crucible of real-world leadership.

As we embark on this journey together, remember that Stoic leadership is not a passive philosophy. It is a call to action, a summons to lead with purpose, wisdom, and unwavering resolve. Through the pages that follow, we will dive further into the crucible of Stoicism in action, forging leaders who not only weather the storms of change, but emerge stronger, wiser, and more impactful than ever before. It is time to embrace the mantle of Stoic leadership and leave an indelible mark on the world.

In the intricacy of leadership, one must be equipped to navigate through a myriad of challenges. From the new territories of the business world to the intricate dynamics of community and home, the Stoic leader is a beacon of calm amidst the storm. This book offers a precise roadmap, drawn from real-life experiences, to empower leaders at every stage of their journey.

For the emerging leader, the path forward can seem treacherous and uncertain. Yet, it is in this crucible that true leaders are forged. Drawing on the sagacity of seasoned Stoic leaders, this section imparts invaluable strategies tailored to those taking their first steps in the realm of influence. It is a guide, a mentor, and a companion for those venturing into new territory.

The seasoned leader, having weathered countless storms, stands on the precipice of greatness. Yet, even the most experienced can find solace and wisdom in the enduring principles of Stoicism. Through the lens of battle-hardened leaders, this section unveils advanced tactics, enabling those with years of experience to refine their approach and elevate their impact.

As we move further into the heart of Stoic leadership, remember that mastery is not an endpoint, but a continuous journey. It is a relentless pursuit of excellence, a commitment to growth, and an unwavering dedication to the principles that guide us. Together, we will navigate the complexities of leadership, drawing strength from the age-old wisdom of Stoicism, and emerge as leaders who not only persevere, but thrive in the face of adversity. It is time to seize the reins of leadership with confidence, wisdom, and the unyielding spirit of a Stoic.

In the crucible of leadership, decisions are the crucible where outcomes are shaped. This book is dedicated to honing the art of decision-making with a Stoic lens. Drawing from real-life situations, we dissect the anatomy of impactful choices, exploring how Stoic principles guide leaders towards decisions that stand the test of time.

Leadership is not solitary; it thrives on effective communication and the power to inspire and guide. This section offers practical tactics for communicating with clarity, empathy, and impact. Through vivid anecdotes, we illuminate how Stoicism empowers leaders to connect, persuade, and mobilize their teams towards shared objectives.

Conflict is an inevitable facet of leadership. Yet, Stoicism provides a steadfast compass for leaders facing discord. In this section, we look into strategies for resolving conflicts with virtue and integrity. Through real-life examples, we demonstrate how Stoic leaders transform discord into opportunities for growth and understanding.

A thriving organization, community, or household is one that embraces growth and development. Here, we explore how Stoic leaders foster environments that nurture continuous improvement and learning. Drawing from practical experiences, we reveal the tactics that empower leaders to cultivate cultures of growth, where individuals flourish and collective goals are achieved.

Leadership transcends the present moment; it leaves an indelible mark on the fabric of existence. In this final section, we reflect on the enduring legacy of Stoic leaders. Through poignant narratives, we showcase how Stoicism empowers leaders to leave a profound, lasting impact on their organizations, communities, and families.

As we embark on this journey together, remember that leadership is not a solitary pursuit. It is a collective endeavor, one that draws strength from the wisdom of the ages and the experiences of those who have come before us. With Stoicism as our guiding light, we stand poised to lead with purpose, integrity, and an unwavering commitment to the greater good. Let us forge ahead, to the next chapter for the strategies which will leave a legacy of Stoic leadership that inspires and guides generations to come.

Chapter 1

The Stoic CEO

*I*n the realm of corporate leadership, the role of a CEO is a constant juggling act of responsibilities, decisions, and strategies. Being A CEO is certainly the most integral part of every corporation since he/she is the one who has to call the shots. It is a like a mind which has control over the whole body i.e., the company in this situation.

This means that if the CEO's life or mental health is affected by any troubling thought or worry, the whole corporation shall suffer the consequences. This is why it is significant for a CEO to be impartial and steadfast in his/her decision-making. A CEO must embody emotional regularity, mental strength and undisputed resolve to come up with unbiased opinions on matters which pertains to the company.

For a CEO, each day unfolds with a rhythm, a cadence shaped by a deliberate routine and a steadfast adherence to principles. In this chapter, we will look into the life of a CEO and understand how stoicism can help daily routine make the job more efficient.

It is not an unknown fact that most people who get successful have a strict sleeping regime which helps them wake up at an oddly early hour in the morning. So, most CEOs generally wake up before the dawn breaks. It is advised by medical professionals and it is practiced by other professionals.

As the first light of dawn graces the horizon, a stoic CEO will step into the day with purpose and a predetermined to-do list to help him get by all his daily duties.

A predawn ritual should mark the beginning, emphasizing the importance of setting the tone for the hours ahead. This early regimen includes exercise, meditation, and reflection, nurturing both body and mind for the challenges that await. It's a practice in discipline, a quiet preparation for the daily demands that lie ahead.

With the sunrise, the CEO's day springs into motion. The inbox fills with emails, reports, and memos - each a decision waiting to be made. The office becomes a hive of activity, a space where strategies are forged, alliances are strengthened, and visions are clarified. A stoic CEO navigates this space with a calm demeanor, listening intently and offering guidance that is measured and sagacious.

Decisions, both significant and minor, punctuate the day. From major business moves to personnel matters, the weight of these choices is palpable. Yet, the CEO approaches each one with a resolute commitment to the organization's mission and values. CEO's understand that decisions have consequences, and the impact of choices resonates far beyond the confines of the boardroom.

Amidst the flurry of activity, moments of solitude become essential. This is where stoicism comes in and assists whenever the information begins overburdening his mind. The stoic CEO will seek out a sanctuary of stillness, a space where the noise of the world is muted, and contemplation reigns supreme. Here, quietly sifting through the complexities of responsibilities, helps find clarity in the midst of potentially overbearing demands. Meanwhile the CEO who does not practice at least some principles of stoicism can become anxious and possibly feel overwhelmed due to the mountain of data requiring intellectual processing.

A CEO's day is a testament to the balance between vision and pragmatism recognizing the delicate dance between short-term gains and long-term aspirations. It's an understanding that success is not a sprint, but a marathon, and each step must be measured with purpose.

As the day draws to a close, the Stoic CEO emerges from the office, bearing the weight of responsibilities with a quiet grace. Meanwhile any other person would have taken these burdening thoughts back to their home, a stoic CEO will leave them at the workplace. Their demeanor must remain resolute, a product of years of experience. They leave not with weariness, but with a sense of fulfillment, knowing that the decisions made today are the building blocks of tomorrow's successes.

In the world of corporate leadership, the stoic CEO serves as an example of strength, embodying a commitment to lead with wisdom and equanimity. Their routine must consist of discipline, discernment, and an unwavering adherence to guiding principles.

Now let's delve deeper into the mind of a stoic CEO.

In today's rapidly evolving business landscape, CEOs face an increasingly challenging task: making critical judgments amidst uncertainty. The demand for astute decision-making has never been higher, as CEOs grapple with a lack of predefined playbooks and navigate high-stakes situations on a daily basis.

The ramifications of erroneous choices are profound. CEOs find themselves under intense scrutiny from shareholders, customers, communities, and regulators alike. Even seemingly inconspicuous decisions can trigger significant repercussions. Striking a delicate balance to satisfy diverse stakeholder groups has become an essential skill for CEOs.

Consider the sustainability agenda, for instance. Crafting an effective plan to reduce emissions involves navigating multifaceted complexities and engaging with a spectrum of stakeholders to foster momentum. Simultaneously, CEOs must address resistance, requiring them to navigate through a diverse array of expectations to chart a path forward. While perfection in decision-making remains elusive, stoic CEOs embody three key traits that enhance their ability to make sound judgments:

Firstly, as the complexity of the CEO's role expands, so does the need for receptivity to fresh perspectives. In a swiftly changing landscape, conventional fixes no longer suffice. Solutions now emerge in various forms, sometimes from unexpected sources.

Secondly, CEOs who excel in making complex decisions exhibit high levels of curiosity and empathy. This enables them to comprehend issues from diverse vantage points and thoroughly assess all potential outcomes and trade-offs before arriving at a decision.

Thirdly, they do not shy away from making unpopular or confrontational decisions. They actively manage stakeholder expectations in collaboration with the board, particularly the chairperson.

The days of a CEO adopting a unilateral, command-and-control approach to decision-making are behind us. The archetype of the maverick "Lone Ranger" CEO has waned, giving way to the imperative of CEOs acting as a "Collaborator in Chief."

CEOs who navigate high-stakes decisions in complex environments are comfortable admitting that they do not possess all the answers. They recognize that soliciting a diverse range of viewpoints from across the organization leads to a more comprehensive understanding of potential blind spots and, subsequently, better decisions.

This necessitates building leadership teams that offer complementary capabilities, drawing upon diversity of experience, perspective, and cognitive abilities. It also underscores the importance of proactive collaboration with the board on challenging issues, as well as with external stakeholders such as regulators and local communities.

Complex decisions often carry a significant emotional weight. Attempting to make decisions in the absence of complete information can leave one feeling vulnerable and exposed. This pressure and stress can lead to extreme behaviors that undermine the ability to make confident judgment calls.

CEOs who excel in complex decision-making do not shy away from their emotions. They tune into them without allowing them to overpower their judgment. They demonstrate high emotional intelligence, ensuring they avoid impulsive reactions and remain receptive to new ideas. When circumstances change or new information emerges, they respond with agility, managing unexpected developments with maturity and composure.

In conclusion, CEOs are encouraged to foster a culture that avoids groupthink, prioritizes team effectiveness, and cultivates strong relationships with their board members. Embracing emotional awareness and understanding personal limits are critical steps toward becoming effective and stoic decision-makers.

Stoicism and the art of Decision-Making: A CEO's Path to Resolute Leadership

In the fast-paced world of corporate leadership, CEOs are tasked with making decisions that carry significant consequences for their organizations. The ability to navigate through complexity, uncertainty, and high-stakes situations is paramount. Stoicism, an ancient philosophy, offers a powerful framework that equips CEOs with the mental strength and clarity needed to make sound judgments.

Now let's elaborate on how stoicism enhances a CEO's decision-making skills, providing insights into its practical applications and benefits in the modern corporate landscape.

Stoicism, founded in ancient Greece by philosophers like Zeno of Citium, is a philosophy that emphasized personal virtue, rationality, and self-discipline as the keys to leading a virtuous and fulfilling life. At its core, stoicism teaches individuals to focus on what they can control, accept what they cannot, and cultivate an inner calm in the face of external circumstances. These principles form a solid foundation for enhancing decision-making skills.

One of the fundamental teachings of stoicism is the mastery of one's emotions. This ability to maintain emotional equilibrium, especially in high-pressure situations, is a cornerstone of effective decision-making for CEOs. By training themselves to acknowledge and accept their emotions without being controlled by them, CEOs can approach decision-making with a clarity and rationality of mind not generally otherwise possible...

Negative visualization involves contemplating potential challenges or setbacks, preparing the mind for adversity. This practice allows CEOs to anticipate obstacles in decision-making and devise strategies to mitigate them.

Stoicism teaches that there are things within our control (our thoughts, actions, and responses) and things beyond our control (external events, other's opinions). CEOs who fully internalize this concept can focus their energy on making decisions based on what they can influence, rather than being paralyzed by external and generally uncontrollable factors.

Stoicism encourages rationality as a guiding force in decision-making. By employing logical thinking and maintaining a clear perspective, CEOs can approach complex choices with greater efficacy.

Stoicism emphasizes the importance of withholding immediate judgments and critically assessing situations before making decisions. This discipline of assent helps CEOs avoid hasty or impulsive choices.

CEOs can benefit from the stoic practice of mentally preparing for potential adversities associated with their decisions. This proactive approach fosters a thorough consideration of all possible outcomes and enhances decision-making acumen.

Stoicism teaches individuals to embrace adversity as an inevitable part of life. CEOs, often faced with high-stakes decisions in volatile environments, can draw strength from this philosophy to approach uncertainty with resilience and composure.

Stoicism encourages individuals to not only accept challenges but to embrace them as opportunities for growth and learning. CEOs who adopt this mindset can transform setbacks into catalysts for better decision-making.

By accepting the reality of a situation, CEOs can free themselves from the burden of futile resistance. This acceptance allows them to focus on finding effective solutions rather than dwelling on uncontrollable circumstances.

Stoicism places a strong emphasis on living a life of virtue and integrity. For CEOs, aligning decision-making with ethical principles is essential for long-term success and organizational well-being.

Stoicism places a strong emphasis on living a life of virtue and integrity. For CEOs, aligning decisions with ethical principles is essential for long-term success and organizational well-being.

Wisdom, a central virtue in stoicism, entails making decisions guided by rationality, fairness, and the greater good. CEOs who prioritize wisdom in their decision-making process, contribute to a culture of ethical leadership within their organizations.

Eudaimonia, often translated as "flourishing" or "fulfillment," is the ultimate goal of stoic life. CEOs who make decisions in alignment with eudaimonic principles prioritize the well-being and flourishing of their organizations, employees, and stakeholders.

Stoicism, with its emphasis on emotional resilience, rationality, adversity acceptance, and ethical leadership, provides a robust framework for enhancing a CEO's decision-making skills. By integrating stoic principles into their leadership approach, CEOs can navigate complex challenges with wisdom, clarity, and integrity. In an ever-evolving corporate landscape, the stoic CEO stands poised to make decisions that not only drive organizational success but also fosters a culture of virtue and resilience.

Even though stoicism is an ancient philosophy rooted in principles of virtue, rationality, and self-discipline, it has still found resonance in the modern world of business and leadership. Let's explore the lives and decisions of CEOs and leaders who have leveraged stoicism to navigate the complexities of the corporate landscape as well as political landscapes. Using real-world examples, we gain an understanding of how these leaders have applied stoic principles to enhance their decision-making, resilience, and ethical leadership.

Marcus Aurelius

Marcus Aurelius, a renowned Roman Emperor from 161 to 180 AD, is a quintessential example of a leader who led with stoic principles in his rule. His personal writings, collected in "Meditations," offer profound insights into his stoic philosophy and its application in governance.

As the ruler of an empire beset by societal unrest, military conflicts, and political intrigue, Marcus turned to the teachings of Stoicism to find solace and guidance to calm his mind. Marcus Aurelius faced a whole range of challenges during his reign, including political turmoil, external threats and internal conflict. His stoic mindset allowed him to maintain composure and make rational decisions even in the midst of chaos. Through the lens of Stoicism, Marcus Aurelius navigated the turbulent seas of his reign with a steadfast commitment to virtue and was successful in upholding his Stoic principles of virtue and justice even in his governance. All of his decisions were guided by a sense of duty to the welfare of the Roman Empire and its citizens.

Seneca the Younger

Seneca is a prominent Stoic philosopher. He served as an advisor to Emperor Nero in the first century AD and his writings, particularly his letters to a young friend, provide invaluable insights into how he applied stoic principles to navigate the complex world of power and influence.

Seneca grappled with the challenges of wealth and influence, often advocating for simplicity and moderation. His stoic perspective enabled him to use his position for the betterment of society, rather than succumbing to excess and opulence.

Seneca's contemplation of death, a core stoic practice, influenced his approach to decision-making. He acknowledged the impermanence of life and used this awareness to make choices that aligned with his values and principles.

Jack Dorsey: Twitter's Stoic CEO

Jack Dorsey, the co-founder and former CEO of Twitter, has openly embraced stoicism as a guiding philosophy in the contemporary business world. His adoption of stoic principles is evident in all of his decision and even in the way he leads his corporation

Dorsey emphasizes the importance of mindfulness and intentionality in his daily routine. This aligns with stoic practices of self-awareness and deliberate action, allowing him to make decisions with clarity and purpose.

Dorsey's stoic mindset is evident in his approach to adversity and criticism. Rather than being swayed by external opinions, he maintains composure and focuses on what he can control, a key tenet of stoicism.

Indra Nooyi

Indra Nooyi, former CEO of PepsiCo, is well known for her disciplined leadership style and strategic decision-making. Her approach to leadership based on Stoicism played a pivotal role in her success and impact on the company.

Nooyi's measured approach to decision-making reflects the stoic discipline of assent. She carefully weighs options, considers potential outcomes, and refrains from impulsive choices, ensuring decisions are grounded in rationality.

Nooyi's commitment to ethical leadership aligns with stoic principles of virtue. Her decisions prioritized the long-term sustainability and well-being of PepsiCo, reflecting a dedication to the greater good.

The examples of Marcus Aurelius, Seneca, Jack Dorsey, and Indra Nooyi highlight the diverse ways in which stoicism can be applied in the realm of leadership. These CEOs leveraged stoic principles to navigate adversity, make rational decisions, practice ethical leadership, and maintain composure in the face of challenges. Their experiences serve as a testament to the enduring relevance of stoicism in the modern world of business and leadership, offering valuable insights for leaders seeking to cultivate resilience, wisdom, and ethical strength. By integrating stoicism into their leadership philosophy, CEOs can forge a path towards enduring success and virtuous leadership.

The Stoic CEO

Balancing Work and Private Life with Wisdom and Virtue

For CEOs, achieving a harmonious balance between professional responsibilities and personal well-being is a formidable challenge. The principles of stoicism offer a timeless framework for navigating this delicate equilibrium. The next part explores how stoic philosophy can guide CEOs in managing their work-life balance with wisdom, virtue, and resilience.

Stoicism emphasizes distinguishing between factors within our control and those beyond it. Applying this principle allows CEOs to approach their work-life balance with a clear perspective.

CEOs can concentrate their efforts on factors such as time management, setting priorities, and establishing boundaries. This approach helps prevent burnout and maintain a healthier work-life equilibrium.

Stoicism encourages CEOs to accept that there will always be unforeseen circumstances and unexpected demands. By acknowledging this reality, they can adapt with composure and make decisions guided by virtue.

Stoicism emphasizes the importance of being present in each moment. This practice fosters a deeper connection to both professional responsibilities and personal life.

CEOs can apply stoic mindfulness techniques to fully engage in their work, allowing for more efficient and effective decision-making. This focused approach enhances productivity without sacrificing quality.

Being present in personal relationships is equally important. By dedicating undivided attention to loved ones, CEOs can nurture meaningful connections and derive fulfillment from their private lives.

Stoicism emphasizes living a life of virtue and aligning decisions with ethical principles. CEOs can apply this principle to prioritize their responsibilities in both professional and personal domains.

CEOs can assess their priorities based on virtues like wisdom, justice, and temperance. This ensures that their choices reflect ethical considerations, fostering a sense of fulfillment and integrity.

Stoicism encourages CEOs to uphold commitments and responsibilities in both spheres with integrity. This means setting realistic expectations, communicating effectively, and honoring one's word.

Stoicism equips CEOs with the tools to navigate adversity with grace and strength. This resilience is important in maintaining balance amidst the inevitable challenges of leadership.

Stoicism teaches that challenges are an inherent part of life. CEOs can view difficulties as opportunities for personal and professional development, cultivating a mindset of continuous improvement.

When faced with unexpected crises, stoic CEOs can draw on their inner strength to approach the situation with calm and rationality. This centered approach allows for more effective problem-solving.

Balancing work and private life as a stoic CEO are ongoing practices that require self-awareness, discipline, and a commitment to virtue. By embracing the principles of stoicism,

CEOs can navigate the complexities of their roles with wisdom, integrity, and resilience. This holistic approach not only fosters a healthier work-life equilibrium but also cultivates a sense of fulfillment and purpose in both professional and personal endeavors. In living as stoic CEOs, leaders can inspire their teams, families, and communities with a model of balanced and virtuous leadership.

Chapter 2

The Aspiring Managers

*T*he lives of remarkable leaders throughout this situation bear witness to the resonance of Stoic philosophy. We will read about the long-term effects of stoic principles in this chapter, and also how they could help aspiring leaders and teach them how to be stoic leaders.

Stoicism's central tenet is that people have the innate ability to develop virtue and inner strength regardless of their external environment. It teaches us that mental control and the capacity to face life's obstacles with composure and intention are the sources of true freedom. This fundamental idea has supported innumerable leaders during difficult times of struggle and suffering.

There are several leaders of the world who have served their nation or their company under the guise of stoicism to later renowned all over the world.

One of those renowned leaders is Admiral James Stockdale, a decorated Vietnam War veteran who embodied the essence of Stoic resilience in the face of unimaginable adversity. Shot down over enemy territory and subsequently held captive as a prisoner of war, Stockdale drew upon the teachings of Epictetus and Seneca to endure years of brutal captivity. His unwavering focus on what he could control, his unyielding resolve to maintain his dignity, and his unwavering sense of duty to his fellow prisoners exemplified the Stoic ethos in its purest form.

In the realm of entrepreneurship and innovation, Steve Jobs emerges as a modern-day exemplar of stoic-inspired leadership. Jobs, co-founder of Apple Inc., transformed the technology sector with his innovative thinking, unwavering pursuit of perfection, and unshakable dedication to his ideals. Jobs embodied the Stoic virtue of wisdom throughout his triumphs and sorrows, realizing that genuine success lay not in immediate profits, but in the long-term consequences of his activities.

These examples demonstrate Stoicism's lasting significance in the area of leadership. They demonstrate that the essence of leadership rests not in the lack of problems, but in how one faces and overcomes them. Through the prism of Stoic philosophy, these leaders found strength in adversity, clarity in complexity, and purpose in their pursuits.

As we continue to explore the topic of Stoic-inspired leadership, let's keep in mind that the lessons taken from these stories are not relegated to the pages of hiSituation, but are living principles that can guide us in our own leadership journeys. In the following part of this book, we will go deeper into the importance of inexperience and new viewpoints, the necessity of acting as the leader one desires to be, and the importance of careful preparation for leadership roles.

In doing so, we will discover the timeless wisdom that Stoicism imparts to leaders, affirming that inexperience is a wellspring of untapped potential, that authentic leadership emerges from embodying one's ideals, and that true leaders are forged through a deliberate and continuous process of self-mastery. We will find, via the lens of Stoicism, that the path to leadership is a journey of growth, resilience, and unshakable purpose.

These success tales all have one thing in common: a dedication to Stoic principles in the face of hardship. They demonstrate that leadership is about tackling obstacles with courage, intelligence, and integrity rather than avoiding them. These leaders understood the value of inexperience and fresh perspectives, acted like the leaders they aspired to be, and prepared diligently for their roles.

The takeaway from these stories is clear: inexperience should not be seen as a hindrance, but rather as an opportunity for growth and innovation. By embracing Stoic principles, aspiring leaders can navigate the complexities of their roles with grace and resilience. They can lead with purpose, inspire their teams, and ultimately leave a lasting legacy.

The following are the four characteristics which aspiring manager should embody to be a success Inexperience is often undervalued in the pursuit of leadership roles. Many people believe that only seasoned veterans are qualified to lead, yet this overlooks the potential of those with fresh insights. When you are new to a profession or a role, you bring a fresh perspective to the table. You haven't been shaped by the established norms and routines. This can be and usually is, a tremendous asset.

Imagine a person who has no preconceived beliefs and is not constrained by the thoughts of "how things have always been done." They are not burdened by the weight of previous failures and blunders. Instead, they approach problems with a blank slate, an open mind, and a desire to develop creative solutions.

Inexperience grants the freedom to question without hesitation. It allows for the exploration of unconventional ideas. While seasoned leaders might be tethered to tried-and-true methods, the aspiring leader can think beyond these boundaries. They can see potential opportunity where others may only see obstacles.

Furthermore, fresh perspectives often bring a keen sense of empathy. The newcomer is more attuned to the struggles and concerns of those still in the trenches. They remember what it's like to grapple with the complexities of a role or a task. This empathy can foster a stronger, more cohesive team.

To truly harness the value of inexperience, one must resist the urge to conform too quickly. Embrace the questions and the uncertainty. Use them as fuel for creative thinking and problem-solving. Recognize that your lack of experience is not a deficiency, but a unique strength.

To become a leader, it is necessary to first learn to lead oneself. Stoicism, a philosophy that emphasizes self-mastery and inner strength, is founded on this principle. Aspiring leaders should consider this, understanding that they must embody the qualities they seek in those they wish to lead.

The first step is to identify the type of leader you want to be. Consider the values, characteristics, and principles that you hold dear. Are you drawn to leaders who exude confidence, integrity, and empathy? Do you admire people who make decisions with purpose and clarity?

Once you've identified these characteristics, it's time to put them to use in your own life. This does not imply acting confidently or imitating the actions of established leaders. It means internalizing these qualities and allowing them to guide your actions authentically.

Consider integrity, for example. A leader with integrity is honest, reliable, and principled. To embody this trait, you must hold yourself to the highest ethical standards. Be transparent in your actions and decisions. Recognize and accept responsibility for your mistakes. This not only earns you the respect of your peers, but it also serves as a model for those who look to you for advice.

Confidence is another important aspect of leadership. This doesn't mean projecting an air of invincibility, but rather having faith in your abilities and decisions. It means acknowledging your strengths while remaining open to growth and improvement. It's about taking calculated risks and confronting challenges head on, knowing you're capable of overcoming them.

Leadership requires empathy, which cannot be overstated. It involves truly understanding the perspectives and emotions of those you lead. It requires active listening, genuine concern for others, and the willingness to put yourself in their shoes. You foster a culture of trust and collaboration within your team by demonstrating empathy.

When it comes to acting like the leader you want to be, consistency is essential. It is not enough to display these qualities on occasion; they must be woven into the fabric of your personality. Every day, not just when it's convenient, your team should be able to count on you to lead with integrity, confidence, and empathy.

Finally, keep in mind that leadership is a process, not a destination. It is an ongoing journey of development and self-improvement. Embrace challenges as opportunities to refine your leadership skills. Seek out feedback from those around you and be open to learning from both successes and failures.

In conclusion, acting like the leader you aspire to be is not about imitation, but about internalization. It is about embodying the qualities and principles that you value and allowing them to guide your actions authentically. You not only set a good example for others, but you also pave the way for your own development and success as a leader.

In the pursuit of leadership, preparation is paramount. True leaders, according to Stoicism, are created through deliberate practice and continuous self-improvement. Preparing in advance for a leadership role is laying the groundwork for success, ensuring that when the opportunity arises, you are ready to step into the role with confidence and competence.

Self-awareness is the first step in preparation. Take the time to evaluate your own strengths, weaknesses, and areas for improvement. Understand your values, principles, and guiding philosophies, as they will shape your leadership style. This self-awareness will serve as a compass for you as a leader, guiding your decisions and actions.

Next, cultivate a growth mindset. Recognize that leadership is a journey of continuous learning and development. Embrace challenges and setbacks as opportunities for growth, rather than obstacles to be avoided. Seek out new knowledge, skills, and perspectives that will enhance your effectiveness as a leader.

Networking and building relationships are also important aspects of preparation. Connect with mentors, peers, and other professionals who can provide guidance, support, and insightful advice. As you progress in your leadership journey, these relationships can provide invaluable mentorship, constructive feedback, and a network of support.

Furthermore, seek out opportunities to take on leadership responsibilities, even in smaller capacities. This could involve leading a project, volunteering for a leadership role within an organization, or taking the initiative to mentor others. These experiences will not only allow you to practice and refine your leadership skills but also demonstrate your readiness for larger roles to those around you.

Time management and organizational skills are vital for any leader. Develop systems and strategies to effectively manage your time, prioritize tasks, and delegate responsibilities when necessary. A well-organized leader is better equipped to handle the demands and complexities of leadership roles.

Additionally, cultivate resilience and emotional intelligence. Leadership frequently entails navigating difficult situations, making difficult decisions, and managing conflicts. Effective leadership requires the ability to remain calm under pressure and empathize with the emotions of others.

Finally, never underestimate the power of self-control. Develop the habits and routines that will help you grow as a leader. Setting clear goals, maintaining a strong work ethic, and remaining committed to your personal and professional development are all examples of this.

In conclusion, preparing for leadership roles in advance is a deliberate and ongoing process. Self-awareness, a growth mindset, relationship building, practical experience, honing organizational skills, developing emotional intelligence, and practicing self-discipline are all required. By taking these steps, you establish yourself as a capable and confident leader, ready to seize any opportunity that presents itself.

We discover a common thread that transcends time and circumstance when we examine the stories of leaders who have embraced Stoic principles. It is a thread woven with the virtues of wisdom, courage, and integrity, a thread that bears witness to Stoicism's enduring power in the realm of leadership.

Now that we have learned the characteristics for a successful stoic manager. Let's learn the principles based on stoicism which one should follow to be aligned with his vision.

"The quality of your thoughts shapes the happiness of your life."

Marcus Aurelius

Musonius Rufus spelled it out: a true leader's main job is looking out for their people. It's on us to shield them and ensure they thrive under our guidance. To pull that off, we need to dig deeper than surface-level virtues and principles.

Start with some self-awareness. Challenge your thinking, ask questions, meditate, and read. It's a solid kickoff.

Musonius Rufus handed down four core virtues for a king, and they're still gold for today's leaders.

Being just and fair isn't just a duty—it's a must for leading strong. You've got to be a keen judge of what's right and what's not, so your team gets what they've earned. That's why trust in modern leaders is shaky. Too many have been burned by those who should've had their back.

A leader needs to be just to uphold justice. Dive into the nature of fairness to keep your standards high.

Leading calls for self-control. Set the example for your team. Keeping a lid on recklessness prevents disaster. Before you expect discipline from others, you've got to live it.

Stoicism teaches us to rise above cravings and emotions. Leaders need to be resolute and decisive, not just reacting to situations. It's about simplicity, self-awareness, and tact. These lay the foundation for a disciplined, well-mannered workplace, molding character and behavior.

Live with dignity. Show the way.

Courage isn't the absence of fear—it's moving forward despite it. Many fear failure and dodge challenges, but that's a dead end. Success isn't avoiding failure; it's getting back up, it's making lemonade.

Wisdom's your compass for handling disputes and making smart choices. The media's a wild ride, so it's on us to sift through the noise and focus on the facts. Logic beats emotional arguments, every time.

Leaders grasp the stakes. We aim for near-perfection in our thoughts, words, and actions. We know perfection's out of reach, but pushing for a higher standard keeps us leading strong.

You'll find these four virtues echoing through the next four principles.

Life's full of things out of our grasp. We can't change it all, but we can change how we see it. Worrying about what's beyond your reach won't get you far. Watch your emotions, especially when things don't go as planned. Stay aware and use logic to steer your course.

Stoics aren't unfeeling—they're just wise to the fact that emotions aren't the best compass. Understanding your feelings sharpens your judgment. It builds intuition, letting you know when to push, pause, step back, or recharge for the next challenge.

Quit stressing about the could-haves and focus on making things right.

Earn your team's trust. Show them how it's done. Embrace action and back your team when you delegate. Set the goals, know what's needed, and lead the way.

Stoic leaders aren't perfect, and they know it. They act as needed because they understand what's on the line, whether they win or lose. As Jarie Bolander says, they know their success rides on their team's hard work—and they don't take that for granted.

Stoicism teaches gratitude, humility, ownership, and responsibility. Give credit where and when it's due. Make sure your team knows you value them and their achievements. Don't swipe credit for their sweat, and own up to both your team's victories and losses. Support and empower them to be their best. Treat them with respect and kindness—they all deserve that.

Happiness isn't about chasing stuff and situations. It's about how you face life and make the most of it. We don't always get a winning hand, but with the right moves, we can still come out a winner.

Failures are chances to grow. Stoics get it—worrying about failure guarantees it. They're not scared of failing because they know something scarier: staying down after a fall.

Diversity and inclusion are in demand. Empathy, understanding others' viewpoints, is a must for leaders. The more you get where others are coming from, the stronger your bonds of trust and respect.

These are vital for lifting spirits and engagement in the workplace, and they matter in personal relationships too. Skip the empathy, and you're just fueling division. We're in a divided world already. Disagree without shutting others down.

Everyone wants to feel valued and heard. Approach differing thoughts with an open mind, and aim for solutions—vastly more empowering than picking fights to prove a point.

Emotions are part of life, but they're not always your best guides. In fact, they often hold you back.

Leaders deal with negative emotions such as stress and anxiety, but Stoic leaders know how to turn them around. Channel your frustrations into motivation and push toward your goals instead of getting sidetracked or discouraged. This isn't about ignoring the tough stuff. It's about facing it head-on and finding your path through the storm, not just looking for silver linings.

Like they say, a king carries his nation's fate on his back. Your success rides on your team, and they rely on you to protect their livelihoods.

Own your business—it's yours. Skip the blame game to dodge fallout from failure. Success isn't just nailing it; it's how you bounce back after falling.

Stoics seize every moment. Reflect on your day. Ask yourself, "How'd I do today? How'd I treat others? Was I better than yesterday? What can I nail today to rock tomorrow?"

Journaling and meditation keep you on track for growth. They remind you of your goal and track your progress. Always push forward, one day at a time.

The journeys of Marcus Aurelius, Admiral James Stockdale, Steve Jobs, and Indra Nooyi illuminate the transformative potential of Stoic philosophy. Through triumphs and tribulations, they demonstrated that leadership is not merely a position, but a way of being – a commitment to leading with purpose, authenticity, and a steadfast adherence to one's principles.

The value of inexperience and fresh perspectives, as we have seen, is often underestimated. Yet, these leaders showed us that a lack of preconceived notions can be a wellspring of innovation and a catalyst for creative problem-solving. It is an opportunity to see beyond the confines of tradition and chart new courses towards success.

Acting as the leader one aspires to be is a genuine commitment to embodying one's ideals, not a ruse. It is a call to set a good example by embodying the values and principles that define effective leadership. Through this authenticity, leaders inspire trust, foster collaboration, and create a culture of excellence.

The imperative of preparing for leadership roles in advance is a call to diligence and self-reflection. It acknowledges that leadership is a continuous journey of growth and self-improvement, rather than a destination. Aspiring leaders position themselves for success when the opportunity arises by cultivating self-awareness, seeking mentorship, and honing their skills.

As we consider these principles, keep in mind that Stoicism is a living philosophy that continues to shape the lives of leaders throughout hiSituation. Its teachings remind us that true leadership goes beyond titles and positions; it is a matter of character, how one responds to challenges, and the impact one leaves behind.

In closing, let us take to heart the Stoic lessons demonstrated by ancient leaders. Let us confidently value our inexperience, act authentically, and diligently prepare for the responsibilities that lie ahead. We not only honor the legacy of Stoic leaders who came before us by doing so, but we also pave the way for a new generation of leaders who lead with wisdom, courage, and unwavering integrity. Lead Strong!

Chapter 3

The First Time Manager

New managers encounter various challenges. Problems arise throughout life. Personal relationships, career success, and self-improvement may provide these challenges. To overcome these hurdles, acknowledge and confront them.

Challenges faced by first-time managers

Managing team members and promoting unity can be difficult. Leadership skills are needed to overcome these challenges. First-time managers may struggle with team building. They may struggle to identify the right team members and give assignments that match their skills. Clear communication and a positive team culture may be difficult for them.

Beyond technical skills, professional success demands other skills. Motivating, communicating, and collaborating with teammates is important. These three interconnected skills create a pleasant workplace where people can grow and succeed. Mastering motivation may motivate team members to achieve goals. Although successful communication enables people to express themselves,

Time management is a major challenge for professionals. Managing a team and their individual tasks makes it harder. Managing multiple tasks efficiently is hard. Work must be prioritized and time-managed. They must understand their tasks, deadlines, and teammates' expectations. Excellent organization and multitasking are essential. Leaders must arrange team meetings, one-on-ones, and mentorship alongside their own duties. Productivity and goal achievement need prioritizing and time management. Time management maximizes daily productivity. This method involves prioritizing to locate and prioritize what matters.

New managers have trouble making decisions. New managers find it hard to make tough decisions and handle problems. Decisions that affect the team, organization, and career are difficult. It requires careful consideration, critical thinking, and assessing outcomes. Rookie managers may also feel pressure to prove themselves and gain team and superior trust through their decisions.

Today's complicated and ever-changing world requires decision-making and ambiguity-handling abilities. These key skills help people solve problems, handle ambiguity, and make decisions that reflect their values and goals. Accepting ambiguity and exercising decision-making can improve resilience, growth, and life outcomes. So, it's vital.

One of the largest professional challenges is assigning tasks while maintaining oversight. Delegation requires planning. Assigning tasks to others ensures efficiency and workload distribution. Work assignment and supervision must be balanced in delegation. Micromanaging every project element can slow it down. First-time managers may struggle to surrender control over past employment. This concern stems from past duties and familiarity.

Effective communication is key for managers. Managers must communicate well to complete their tasks and meet corporate goals. Management can effectively communicate ideas, objectives, and directives to teams to ensure everyone is working toward the same goal. It lets supervisors actively listen. As a new boss, you must communicate better. New managers must communicate well and provide their teams with constructive criticism. To have a pleasant and effective workplace, listen to team members' complaints, ideas, and suggestions. These practices help new managers create strong team ties and encourage open communication and collaboration.

Teamwork requires careful dispute resolution and strong communication. Internal and external team conflicts can stress and hinder teamwork. By resolving conflicts, teams can improve workplace harmony. Teams can struggle to resolve conflict. It involves identifying conflict causes, understanding all parties' feelings, and reaching a consensus. This process requires empathy, openness, and engagement. First-time managers need conflict-resolution skills. In the ever-changing workplace, new managers must handle conflicts gracefully. Improved conflict resolution skills help these managers handle conflicts.

Managers regularly adjust to organizational changes. New strategies, cutting-edge technologies, and approaches may be implemented. Managers must be adaptable and actively incorporate these changes into their everyday operations to lead their people through these changes. They may maintain their teams agile, resilient, and ready for changes by doing so.

Giving team members feedback is difficult in performance review. A fair, accurate, and helpful appraisal requires careful analysis and attention to detail. Managers and leaders must be attentive and empathic because this process might impair team morale and motivation. Performance evaluation is difficult because it requires assessing abilities, knowledge, and talents. This requires knowing each team member's role. Giving constructive feedback and conducting performance reviews needs skill and sensitivity. Feedback impacts motivation, self-esteem, and performance. Thus, handling these situations carefully and providing constructive feedback is important.

Successful management entails creating and communicating team and individual goals. For new managers, this work may be complicated.

Career advancement involves good supervisor connections and upward management. Upward management can advance a career in today's fast-paced business. Building rapport with superiors is important while managing up. Open communication, respect, professionalism, and seeking input and direction are needed. Staff can improve their chances of receiving help and recognition by creating trust and respect with their managers.

Effective upward management entails understanding and supporting supervisors' and company goals.

First-time managers can overcome numerous problems by actively participating in extensive training programs, seeking mentorship from experienced leaders, and genuinely wanting to learn and adapt.

For several important reasons, managers must make impartial decisions. In today's complicated and changing business world, management must make vital decisions that may affect their companies' performance and sustainability. Being neutral and objective when making decisions is essential.

Fairness promotes workplace harmony and efficiency. All employees benefit from impartial judgments. This reduces discrimination and favoritism and increases employee trust, satisfaction and motivation. Fairness helps companies treat all employees equally, regardless of background, gender, color, or other considerations. Everyone has an equal chance to thrive in their careers based on their talents, qualifications, and performance. Fair work settings help employees feel valued and respected since they are appropriately compensated. Motivation and morale boost productivity and job happiness. When they know their work will be objectively assessed, they work harder. Fairness also reduces workplace bias.

Company performance and productivity depend on employee morale. Well-known, fair judgments boost staff morale and management trust. Fair and impartial evaluations promote work cultures, job happiness, and employee retention. Fair decisions build management-employee trust. When heard and their concerns considered, employees develop decision-making confidence. This confidence promotes management's goals and actions, building trust in the organization. Fair judgments affect employee morale.

Legal compliance is improved by impartial organizational decisions. Making fair, labor-law-compliant decisions helps companies avoid legal difficulties. In today's complex legal landscape, where corporations face greater scrutiny and penalties for noncompliance, this is important. Organizations may trust that they are following the law and fulfilling employee promises with impartial options. Fairness and objectivity in decision-making promote ethical behavior and avoid legal dangers. In the end, impartial decision-making protects firms against legal concerns and promotes a terrific work environment where employees feel valued and treated properly, enhancing productivity.

Impartiality creates objectivity, which is important. Being neutral lets people see things objectively. This improves decisions by providing a fuller assessment. Setting aside prejudices allows people to evaluate the situation. This means decisions are based on facts and evidence, not subjective views or preconceptions. Thus, decisions are more likely to be just and sensible. In addition, impartiality ensures that all relevant information is evaluated. Personal biases may drive people only to accept evidence that supports their views. The Situation may be misinterpreted.

A key manager skill is problem-solving. Managers must handle workplace conflicts to ensure harmony and productivity. By making impartial decisions, managers may address challenges. Managers may assess all relevant factors and perspectives without bias when solving problems. That allows people to make rational, unbiased decisions. Managers can ensure their problem-solving efforts focus on the best team or company solution by doing so. Managers who make impartial decisions can resolve problems better. Every company has conflicts, but how they're handled affects morale. Open and productive communication can be fostered by managers who view conflicts objectively. Effective problem-solving and conflict resolution by managers can also help.

Impartiality improves teams. Impartiality creates a welcoming workplace where everyone feels respected and appreciated for their unique contributions. Trust promotes openness and diversity, making it important for collaboration. Knowing their ideas would be considered on merit rather than bias encourages team members to speak up. Fair treatment of team members reduces perceived unfairness-related rage.

Companies must consider reputation. A reputation for impartial decision-making gives organizations a competitive edge. This edge attracts great talent, fosters consumer loyalty, and strengthens partnerships. Fair and impartial decision-making attracts top talent first. Quality workers demand fair and impartial companies in today's competitive labor market. Ethical and fair companies appeal to them. An organization's neutrality delivers a powerful message to potential employees that their achievements will be recognized and rewarded on merit, not bias. A good reputation for fair decision-making increases client trust and loyalty.

In conclusion, impartial decision-making is essential for fair, peaceful, and legal workplaces. Companies can boost their reputation and problem-solving by making impartial decisions. Fair workplaces require impartial decision-making. By treating all employees fairly and without bias, organizations may promote respect. When they feel valued equally, employees are more motivated and engaged, which boosts morale. In addition, fair decision-making helps businesses manage conflicts and problems. Objective judgments make problem-solving easier. In unbiased decision-making, all relevant factors and views are considered.

Stoic management is infusing your style with knowledge, resilience, and tranquility by completely embracing Stoic concepts. By actively incorporating these concepts into your management philosophy, you may create a strong and revolutionary leadership style and begin a personal growth and self-mastery path that will change your career and personal life.

The ability to recognize and control one's emotions and reactions is essential to personal growth. Self-awareness boosts emotional intelligence and enhances personal and professional judgments. Recognizing our emotions and triggers improves our well-being and coping skills. Traditional Greek stoicism emphasizes self-control and emotional intelligence through self-reflection and intros. This profound worldview encourages people to understand their emotions and use their inner force to transcend life's challenges gracefully.

Accepting our inability to control some things is important. By understanding this essential truth, you may eliminate stress and concern from trying to manage everything. Instead, emphasize your influence and power. This perspective shift helps maximize your resources and efforts. You can optimize your potential and achieve your goals by focusing on controllable elements. Use your resources and abilities to succeed by focusing on these areas. You must also accept that some things are beyond your control. Embracing these limits with patience will help you become accepting and adaptive. Try this method to avoid stress and frustration from trying to modify uncontrollable conditions.

Reason and ethics, not emotions or demands, guide rational decision-making. This means people should consider facts, evidence, and ethics while making decisions. Reason and virtue help people make moral choices. Since emotions and other influences can cloud judgment and lead to impulsive or erroneous conclusions, this technique allows for a more objective evaluation. Logical decision-making requires data collection and analysis. Consider the advantages and cons of each option and their likely outcomes.

This ethical framework encourages morality and decision-making. Stoic virtues, including wisdom, courage, justice, and temperance, promote leadership and ethics. Wisdom is the ability to make appropriate decisions based on complete understanding. Wisdom helps managers handle difficult situations and make smart choices for themselves and their followers. Management requires honesty and morality in many areas. This requires adhering to a set of values that guides one's actions despite temptations. Leading with integrity and morality builds trust and respect.

Being resilient implies overcoming barriers and reaching goals. This quality helps personal growth and success. We stay positive and go on after failures with resilience. It helps us adapt, learn, and overcome obstacles. Stoicism, an ancient philosophy that lasts, offers advice on life's challenges. One of its main themes is that recognizing obstacles as fantastic personal growth opportunities can change them. This thinking builds resilience, strength, and self-awareness, making life more meaningful.

This attitude was motivated by Stoic service and humility. Managers may create a pleasant, empowering environment that grows teams and organizations with this strategy. Selflessness and service are essential to servant leadership. Servant managers support their teams without pursuing personal gain or control. They recognize good leadership fosters trust, cooperation, and empathy. Servant leadership requires humility. Managers with humility learn from their teams. They want feedback from followers' diverse perspectives and expertise. Accepting their mistakes and being humble helps servant managers communicate and improve. Also, servant managers value well-being.

Mindfulness and meditation promote health when practiced daily. Spending time on these activities may help you understand your emotions. Focusing on the present without judgment is mindfulness. It enables you to focus on the now rather than the past or future. Meditation reduces stress and improves mental clarity by focusing on the present. Meditation helps the mind relax and focus. This tool can help you make better judgments and handle stressful situations while staying calm using breathwork and other ways.

We communicate clearly so others can comprehend. Honest communication strengthens relationships by building trust. Stoic managers may inspire and encourage their staff while upholding their ideals. These exceptional managers inspire their teams to greatness while staying loyal to their values. Stoic managers navigate the complex management terrain with elegance and wisdom, motivating and guiding their followers with morals. Their unwavering dedication to their values gives their teams purpose and direction.

Stoicism is essential to leading by example. Live your views, don't just talk about them, instead set an example with your actions. It will set a tremendous example. Displaying Stoic values and behaviors encourages others to embrace them. This may greatly impact others in your life who realize the benefits of Stoicism. Try to apply these ideas to your thoughts, words, and actions to show Stoicism's power and wisdom.

Stoics think learning should never end because it helps individuals understand the world. I urge self-education and aggressively pursuing personal and professional growth. Continuous learning and development can boost your skills, knowledge, and abilities. Continuous progress boosts skills and opens doors. Live to learn and be curious.

To establish a unique and extraordinary Stoic management style that stresses knowledge, virtue, resilience, and ethical decision-making, carefully incorporate these timeless Stoic principles into your leadership style.

Managers must avoid being too strict to establish a positive and productive workplace. By balancing discipline and autonomy, managers may boost employee well-being and productivity. There are many effective approaches to striking the delicate and important balance needed for optimal life results. Carefully assessing and applying these methods can help you achieve homeostasis and efficiently manage your time, energy, and resources for well-being and success.

To encourage collaboration and productivity, allow team members to express their opinions, ideas, and concerns freely. Sharing expertise and comments and helping the team achieve is possible through open communication. Share your thoughts, concerns, and opinions without penalties to promote transparency, trust, and respect among team members. A safe and inclusive space where everyone may express their opinions and participate in important debates is essential. By sharing input, we can solve problems, improve processes, and achieve our goals. Say something and be heard. Your advice is appreciated and helpful.

Being flexible and adaptable to conditions and people's needs is valuable. The flexible can tolerate change without becoming overwhelmed or unwilling. It helps us solve new challenges, communicate, and collaborate. Flexibility boosts problem-solving and uncertainty resilience. Thus, adaptability is essential because a one-size-fits-all method may not work.

Delegate work and let your team decide. By empowering your team, you assign duties and encourage ownership and accountability. This allows team members to take on more responsibility and use their expertise to succeed. Encouraging team members to make decisions displays confidence in their skills and initiative. These productive and effective workplaces need to empower employees to own their jobs and contribute to corporate success. Employee ownership inspires them to succeed and feel responsible for the company's goals. Empowered workers are trusted to make decisions and lead at work. This boosts confidence and unleashes talent. Organizations encourage accountability through employee ownership.

Listening to teammates helps you grasp their perspectives. Actively listening displays respect and empathy, fostering open communication and collaboration. Active listening involves words, body language, and expressions. This thorough listening strategy aids comprehension and response. You must listen to others' issues to communicate well. Focus on the speaker and exhibit genuine interest in their words. Hearing words and recognizing the speaker's tone, body language, and emotions is active listening. Many strategies can help you listen actively. Make eye contact with the speaker to indicate attentiveness. A single action can change things drastically.

Clearly communicating your expectations can help your team members understand their jobs. Details are needed to set expectations. Avoid confusing instructions. Set clear goals and steps to attain them. Additionally, team members must know their jobs. Answer queries and concerns. Encourage team members to ask questions and communicate. Clear expectations eliminate strict control, which offers several benefits. Promoting workplace autonomy is an advantage. Avoiding micromanagement and constant monitoring lets people make their own decisions and creates employee self-confidence, motivation and loyalty.

Feedback helps others improve their abilities and performance. Identifying areas for improvement or suggesting alternatives may boost results. Good effort must also be recognized. Timely recognition of achievements boosts morale and improves the workplace. Give constructive criticism, and thanks for support. Positive reinforcement motivates and encourages desired action better than authoritarianism.

Effective managers regulate essential operations while giving their teams the liberty they need to thrive. Coaching and oversight must be balanced with empowering team members to make their own decisions and own their work. This balance management talent requires considerable study and adjustment due to team chemistry and conditions. Mixing things up may foster a productive, collaborative environment where everyone feels valued and motivated. Team or organization micromanagement can hinder creativity and motivation. A boss who over-monitors and supervises work may reduce employee autonomy and decrease productivity.

Managers must accept that management styles change. Learning and adapting your management style will equip you for business's constant change. Management and learning are lifelong. We must seek growth through formal instruction, reading, or accepting team feedback. Encourage open communication and input to make everyone feel valued and included. Accepting feedback demonstrates your commitment to growth and provides new insights to improve decision-making. Being open to feedback means changing your strategy as needed. You want to learn from others and change your approach since you know you can do better. Managers must be adaptable to overcome challenges.

Good connections and a happy atmosphere demand fair and impartial conflict resolution. Peaceful and courteous disagreement resolution in personal, professional, and community settings requires knowledgeable dispute resolution. Calmly resolve conflicts. Staying cool helps individuals assess and agree. Team members should actively support constructive conflict resolution. Team dynamics and productivity depend on this. By promoting constructive conflict resolution, you allow team members to express their differences.

Helping your team balance work and life improves job satisfaction, mental health, and productivity. Focusing on work-life balance shows you care about team members. Self-care, flexible work, and clear work-life boundaries can help.

Managers can improve by reflecting on their management style and its impact on their teams. Examining your management style might help you understand how your decisions affect others. Consider your management style when self-reflecting. Try to connect with teammates, create trust and respect, and motivate others. Consider these elements. We must aggressively seek and accept personal growth and promotion chances. Daring activities and experiences can improve our knowledge, skills, and perspectives, enhancing our lives.

Chapter 4

The Stoic Retail Manager

*R*etail management involves overseeing and coordinating retail operations. Planning, forecasting, merchandising, operations, marketing, and finance are among its duties.

Retail management is a hectic job which involves overseeing a store's inventory, sales, customer service, staff, and finances. Attention to detail, leadership, and retail business understanding are very much needed in this department. Business and profit are the goals of retail management. This entails developing and implementing strategies to boost sales, attract customers, and improve shopping. The function requires various complex tasks for corporate success. Planning, forecasting, merchandising, operations, marketing, and finance are included. All of these are vital to corporate success. Every area requires skill, from careful strategy and trend forecasting to effective merchandising.

Retail managers must develop thorough sales, inventory, and people strategies and estimates. Retail operations rely on plans and predictions for strategic success and ecosystem smoothness. It takes precision, retail expertise, and powerful analytical tools to complete this difficult process. Retail managers meticulously prepare these plans and forecasts to boost corporate profitability and sustainability. To thrive in this fast-changing environment, one must understand the numerous factors involved. These include the complex retail market, customer behavior, and economic developments. Without comprehending these varied elements, it may be difficult to make informed decisions and strategize effectively in this competitive field. Retail workers must prioritize learning and mastering these topics.

A detailed sales estimate helps retail managers plan inventory. Professional managers optimize stock levels, allocate resources, and assure supply chain efficiency at this important retail management stage. Retail managers may maximize income and customer pleasure by using sales prediction data to guide procurement, production, and distribution. Determining inventory size and order timing is key to inventory management. To balance inventories, retail managers must study customer behavior, market dynamics, and buying habits. When managers forecast client demand, they may supply stores with the right products at the right time, enhancing sales. In the background, overstocking lowers store revenues. Overstocking costs money, storage, maintenance, insurance, and depreciation. Overstocked items may become obsolete and unsellable.

Store managers must forecast staffing demands in addition to everyday operations. Retail managers can accurately estimate staffing needs to ensure shop staffing. Retail shop managers must consider many factors to run smoothly and profitably. They prioritize sales predictions. Retail managers can predict sales using past sales, market trends, and customer preferences. They can plan inventory, allocate resources, and make strategic decisions to meet client demand.

Retail managers choose and display merchandise to maximize sales. A merchandising strategy, product assortments, and promotions are needed.

Retail managers need a thorough merchandising strategy to run a store. This approach guides product selection, pricing, placement, and advertising in retail. The plan can help the company grow and flourish. Target market must be considered in strategy. Business goals and target market features can be used to tailor the strategy to maximize its influence and success. After perfecting the merchandising approach, retail managers may confidently produce enticing product assortments. The competent managers can choose a selection of products that match the merchandising plan and satisfy their discerning clients with a clear vision.

Product assortments must meet market needs. By examining customers' preferences and wants, businesses can build a product range that appeals and fits their needs. Personalizing product assortments helps companies boost customer loyalty and sales. Businesses must invest time and effort studying their target market. Retail managers must consider various business-impacting factors while establishing product assortments. Consider product price carefully. Retail managers must balance customer-attracting prices with reliable profit margins. Along with price, product quality matters.

Retail managers must follow market and consumer trends. They can learn what items and services are popular by attentively watching industry trends and assessing market research data. With this insight, businesses may create tailored promotions. Promotions can use a variety of appealing methods to attract and engage customers. Coupons, discounts, and sales events are among these appealing strategies.

Retail managers supervise daily operations, which are important to business success. Many of their operations improve retail efficiency and profitability. Retail managers manage inventory, staff, customer satisfaction, and sales to succeed. These specialists monitor and resolve operational difficulties to assist the company reach its goals and give customers a good shopping experience.

In addition to regular operations, store managers handle inventories. They must minimize surplus stock, avoid shortages, and guarantee the correct products are available at the right time. Retail managers may maximize sales and customer pleasure by monitoring inventory levels and making purchasing, restocking, and merchandising decisions. Keeping a company functioning demands various inventory management tasks.

Retail managers also need to handle customer complaints. They must be able to resolve customer complaints in a fair and timely manner.

Retail managers develop and implement customer-attracting and retention marketing strategies, which are important to success. These may involve advertising, marketing, social media, and loyalty programs. Advertising, PR, and social media marketing are examples. Advertising persuades via TV, radio, print, and online.

Retail managers must develop a comprehensive marketing plan that satisfies market needs and business goals. Know how customers' tastes are changing, how the market works, how your competitors are doing, and how to analyze data to make informed decisions. By communicating with their target market, firms can create trust. You must choose the correct platforms to market anything.

These sources include social media marketing, web ads, print, and TV adverts. These marketing methods help retail managers reach their target audience and build brand awareness. Public relations may also boost their company's image and maintain strong ties with customers.

Store managers oversee the company's finances. This covers budgeting, forecasting, and reporting.

Store managers must prepare a precise budget to manage company money. The budget estimates income and expenses and guides the organization's finances. Retail managers must accurately predict and forecast company finances. Our important job requires us to thoroughly evaluate consumer behavior, market conditions, and industry competition that affect our firm. We may make informed decisions and establish efficient financial plans by monitoring and assessing these factors. This capacity improves strategic thinking and business success by enabling wise business decisions.

Managers of stores also have to tell people who matter about how the business is doing financially. Owners, buyers, and lenders are some examples of these groups.

Managing a store is exciting and challenging. Store managers are vital to society and the economy. Retail management is difficult, yet successful managers improve their communities and businesses.

Retail managers may also hire and train people, create employee policies, and oversee security. Retail managers must multitask and solve unexpected issues.

Daily retail management is hard and underrated. Retail management is demanding and requires constant juggling. From stocking the store properly, Retail managers require particular skills to solve challenges. Retail managers must manage high personnel turnover and client complaints while running profitable stores. Retail management takes guts. Managing regular personnel turnover demands strength and resilience. High staff turnover makes it hard to find and train replacements. This process takes time to identify, hire, and train new hires. Retail managers are known for their stoicism and rapid choices and actions. Stoics advise staying calm to solve life's issues and make everyday decisions. This worldview encourages people to develop inner peace and approach each situation calmly, free from impulsive emotions and external pressures. Stoics utilize equanimity to consider the consequences of their actions and make decisions that represent their values and goals. Stoics can create a leader who is a force on the front lines of any organization by actively using this decision-making style—definitely a "front line" boss.

Retail bosses often struggle as they have several responsibilities and must often solve unexpected issues.

Here are some of the specific difficulties of a retail manager's job:

- Store managers spend long hours on weekends and late at night to secure their stores' success. Due to illness or others missing shifts, workers may be called in at short notice to complete their obligations.
- Retail managers routinely deal with rude or angry consumers. This is difficult since store managers must remain cool and professional when clients are angry.

- Retail managers hire, train, and manage people. Retail managers must train and meet business requirements, making this difficult.

- Managers must keep ahead in the fast-paced, ever-changing retail market. Retail is continually changing, so be open to new trends. No longer does stocking shelves and providing outstanding service define store success.

- Online shopping, mobile apps, and social media have transformed how people shop and interact with businesses. Retail managers must master digital marketing, omnichannel shopping, and data analytics to connect customers and increase sales since many shoppers today are pickier and have greater criteria.

Achieving the ideal balance between cost containment and profitability is a difficult task. It is a delicate dance as retail managers try to stay within a strict budget and give their devoted customers an enjoyable and memorable shopping experience. Successful retail management is defined by striking a balance between the pursuit of customer satisfaction and financial considerations.

Despite the many challenges, becoming a store manager can be quite rewarding. Retail managers affect their dedicated employees and devoted customers. Because they have a unique blend of leadership qualities, business expertise, and a genuine desire to make people happy, these managers can change lives.

Retail managers must be structured, efficient, strong communicators, adaptable, and passionate about retail to succeed.

Stoicism is a philosophy that teaches us how to live a good life by focusing on what we can control and accepting what we cannot control. It can be a valuable philosophy for retail managers, who often face a variety of challenges and stressors.

Here are some of the ways in which retail managers can benefit from stoicism:

Retail managers face unpleasant people, a lot of work, and unexpected issues. Stoicism can assist retail managers to keep calm and focused during difficult times. Understanding that things don't always go as planned and focusing on what they can control helps shop managers relax and perform better.

Instead of being influenced by emotions, stoics make reasoned, logical decisions. Store owners who need to make quick judgments may benefit from this approach. By using this application, users can streamline their decision-making process and save time and energy for other duties. Store owners can boost productivity and efficiency by making quick decisions, improving business results. Stoic principles provide shop managers with a solid framework for serious reflection and deliberate action, resulting in better judgments.

For example, if a retail manager is faced with a difficult decision about whether to discount a product or not, they can use stoic principles to weigh the pros and cons of each option and make the decision that is best for the business in the long run.

Stoicism teaches us to treat others with respect and compassion. This can help retail managers to build better relationships with their employees and customers.

Stoic principles properly applied can help managers solve employee behavior issues and create a peaceful workplace. Stoicism helps managers handle tough conditions. Only we can regulate our ideas, feelings, and actions, according to Stoicism. Stoicism improves self-awareness and emotional intelligence, helping managers negotiate. Many believe supervisors are not required to address employee misconduct swiftly. To tackle the problems, leaders must examine an employee's goals and reasons. This complete understanding helps the supervisor respond kindlier and constructively to the employee's thoughts, feelings, and motives. This understanding creates a more loving and supportive environment and meaningful answers to employee difficulties and growth.

Here are some specific examples of how retail managers can apply stoic principles to their work:

- A rude customer requires the shop manager to remain calm and professional. The store manager may handle the difficult issue with grace and tact, satisfying the customer and upholding the store's standards. A comprehensive approach will prepare the store manager for the hardest situations. The store manager might propose novel solutions by evaluating client needs. This strategy considers current and future client needs. The store manager can boost customer satisfaction via open communication, active listening, and proactivity. This mentality allows the store manager to overcome barriers and exceed customer expectations courageously. Customer satisfaction will be ensured by prompt confirmation of their request or question and feedback. Dedicated and experienced personnel will exceed client expectations and give excellent customer service. These people will diligently build strong, lasting relationships with their valued clients and establish an environment of trust, reliability, and mutual respect, ensuring every engagement is warm, real, and genuine.

- When faced with a difficult decision, a stoic retail manager will weigh the pros and cons of each option carefully before making a decision. They will not make impulsive decisions based on their emotions.

- Stoic retail managers can handle irritable employees. This manager will consider the employee's perspective and why they acted before taking action. This boss understands the importance of a tranquil, supportive, and honored workplace. Stay cool and analyze the pros and cons of several schemes and choices. They recognize that every worker has talents and limitations, and that employers and firms must treat workers' sentiments fairly and professionally. Do not react against an employee or take their rage personally. This promotes healthy communication and a fantastic work culture that values free debate and respect. When dealing with unexpected challenges, the stoic retail manager will remain calm and focused. They will not let the challenges overwhelm them, and they will focus on finding solutions.

- When things do not go according to plan, a stoic retail manager will not dwell on the past. They will accept what has happened and move on to the next task.

Stoicism can improve shop managers' performance and purpose. Epictetus', Seneca's, and Marcus Aurelius' rich legacy can help shop managers lead gracefully and efficiently. Stoicism, which emphasizes inner tranquility and virtue in the face of external challenges, provides valuable insights and practical advice for shop management. Stoicism's practical advice and profound insights help shop managers navigate their demanding and ever-changing professions. To embrace Stoicism, retail managers should follow Stoic ideals.

Discipline and self-awareness offer peace in Stoicism. It encourages us to focus and establish a foundation. Stoicism can help retail managers keep calm in the fast-paced, ever-changing industry. Retail managers may handle unpredictability and succeed with stoicism. Serenity helps people make reasoned decisions without emotion. Store managers gain from stoicism. Zeno of Citium's stoicism genuinely assesses shop management issues.

Stoicism is a philosophy that teaches us to live a good life by focusing on what we can control and accepting what we cannot control. It can be a valuable philosophy for retail managers, who often face a variety of challenges and stressors outside of their control.

There are a number of things that retail managers can do to implement stoicism in their jobs, including:

Mindfulness is a key tenet of stoicism. Mindfulness involves paying attention to the present moment without judgment. This can be helpful for retail managers, who are often juggling multiple tasks and dealing with a variety of distractions.

By practicing mindfulness, retail managers can become more aware of their thoughts, feelings, and bodily sensations. This can help them to stay calm and focused in the face of adversity.

Here are a few tips for practicing mindfulness:

- Take a few minutes each day to sit quietly and focus on your breath. Pay attention to the rise and fall of your chest as you inhale and exhale.
- When you are feeling overwhelmed or stressed, stop and take a few deep breaths. Focus on your breath and try to let go of any negative thoughts or emotions.
- When you are interacting with customers or employees, be mindful of your body language and tone of voice. Make eye contact and listen actively.

Stoicism believes negative ideas are unrealistic and unhelpful to our search for meaning. Retail managers may question these ideas' reasoning. They must question their beliefs and thinking. Individuals can decide if these views are backed by evidence or their imagination by doing so. Retail managers may comprehend their ideas and make rational decisions through self-reflection.

A hardworking store manager may consider, "Maybe I am not adequately skilled or proficient enough to excel in this demanding role." Retail managers must have productive internal dialogue to examine their thoughts and self-perception of inadequacy when introspecting. Questioning their beliefs helps the shop manager decide if their anxieties are justified. In addition to seeking external validation, self-reflection can help people remember their abilities, talents, and accomplishments. Recognizing and recognizing their strengths helps boost self-confidence and resilience to overcome challenges.

By challenging negative thoughts, retail managers can improve their self-confidence and reduce their stress levels.

Here are a few tips for challenging negative thoughts:

- Ask yourself if the thought is rational. Is there any evidence to support the thought?

- Identify the underlying belief. What is the belief that is causing the negative thought?
- Challenge the underlying belief. Is the belief realistic? Is it helpful?
- Replace the negative thought with a more positive and realistic thought.

Stoicism gives significant insight to anyone seeking balance and fulfillment. Stoicism emphasizes controlling what we can and letting go of the rest. This proven philosophy promotes inner serenity and resilience in life's inevitable challenges. Staying positive can help retail managers attract customers and employees. Store managers require character and drive. Be attentive and committed to success.

Shop managers must realize some circumstances are beyond their control. One example is customer behavior. Retail managers can control their own reactions but not client conduct. Excellent customer service requires patience and empathy, especially with challenging customers. Customer service agents may handle difficult situations and meet clients' needs by being patient and empathetic. Staying calm in stressful situations displays professionalism and promotes a harmonious environment for both the customer and the salesperson.

Here are a few tips for focusing on what you can control:

- Identify the things that you can control. This may include your own attitude, your work ethic, your customer service skills, and your preparation for unexpected events.
- Focus your attention on the things that you can control. This means letting go of things that you cannot control, such as the behavior of customers, the actions of competitors, and the state of the economy.
- Take action to improve the things that you can control. This may involve developing new skills, changing your attitude, or creating new processes.

Stoics believe bad things will happen. Retail managers can be prepared for problems by having a plan.

This strategy may include extra money for unanticipated costs, a supply chain backup plan, and a customer complaint procedure.

By being prepared for setbacks, retail managers can reduce the impact of these events on their businesses and their employees.

Here are a few tips for being prepared for setbacks:

- Identify the potential setbacks that your business could face. This may include things like supply chain disruptions, customer complaints, and economic downturns.
- Develop a plan for how you will deal with each potential setback. This plan should be specific and actionable.
- Review and update your plan regularly. The business world is constantly changing, so it is important to make sure that your plan is still relevant.

Stoicism teaches that mistakes are an opportunity to learn and grow. Retail managers can learn from their mistakes by reflecting on what went wrong and how they can do better in the future.

It is important to remember that everyone makes mistakes. The key is to learn from them and avoid making the same mistakes in the future.

Here are a few tips for learning from mistakes:

- Take some time to reflect on what went wrong. What factors contributed to the mistake? What could you have done differently?
- Be honest with yourself about your role in the mistake. Don't try to blame others or make excuses.

- Identify the lessons that you can learn from the experience. What can you do to avoid making the same mistake in the future?
- Develop a plan for improvement. This plan may involve changing your approach to a task, developing new skills, or creating new processes.
- Implement your plan and monitor your progress. Make sure that you are learning from your mistakes and making improvements.

Stoicism is a powerful philosophy that can help retail managers to improve their performance, build better relationships, and live more fulfilling lives. By following the tips above, retail managers can begin to implement stoicism in their jobs and start to see the benefits.

Here are some additional tips for retail managers who want to implement stoicism in their jobs:

- Find a guide who is stoic. Ask someone you know who is silent to be your guide. Someone who knows a lot about stoicism can teach you how to use it in your own life.
- Join a stoic community. There are many stoic communities online and in person. Joining a stoic community can help

you to learn from others and to get support on your journey.

- Read books and articles about stoicism. There are many resources available on stoicism, including books, articles, and online courses. Reading about stoicism can help you to better understand the philosophy and how to apply it to your life.

- Practice stoicism daily. Stoicism improves with practice. Find ways to practice stoicism when dealing with unpleasant clients, making tough decisions, or encountering unforeseen problems.

- Stoicism is a lifelong journey, but it is one that is well worth taking. By following the principles of stoicism, retail managers can improve their performance, build better relationships, and live more fulfilling lives.

Stoicism can be a valuable tool for retail managers. By implementing stoic principles, retail managers can reduce stress, improve their decision-making, and increase productivity. Stoicism can also help retail managers create a more positive work environment, improve employee morale, and enhance customer service.

Stoicism's intellectual and practical basis may help retail managers lead with empathy and understanding, among other benefits. Stoicism develops self-awareness and emotional intelligence, helping retail managers interact with employees. Empathy is the wonderful and fundamentally human ability to comprehend, accept, and empathize with others' emotions and experiences. This complex process lets us see others' pleasures, sufferings, accomplishments, and problems. By interacting with customers more deeply, retail managers may provide excellent service and unique experiences that boost customer loyalty. Great retail managers make actual connections in the ever-changing retail environment.

Stoicism can help retail managers develop empathy by teaching them to:

- **Suspend judgment:** Stoicism teaches that it is important to suspend judgment and try to see things from the perspective of others. This can help retail managers understand why customers or employees are behaving in a certain way.
- **Listen actively**: Stoicism teaches the importance of active listening. Active listening involves paying attention to what

the other person is saying, both verbally and nonverbally. This can help retail managers build rapport with customers and employees.

- **Put themselves in others' shoes:** Stoicism teaches that it is important to put oneself in the shoes of others which will certainly help retail managers understand the challenges and struggles that their employees and customers are facing.

- Retail managers may foster a healthy, productive workplace by establishing empathy. Understanding and sharing another's feelings can change retail relations. Among Stoicism's numerous benefits, social media can help companies create better customer relationships. Companies may establish community and engage customers on Facebook, Instagram, and X by actively interacting. Companies can demonstrate customer satisfaction and outstanding service by responding to comments, messages, and reviews. This personalized strategy boosts sales, brings repeat business, and client satisfaction.

Here are a few examples of how stoicism can be applied in retail management:

- A customer is angry and yelling at a cashier. A stoic retail manager would:
    - Remain calm and avoid reacting emotionally.
    - Listen to the customer's complaint without interrupting.
    - Try to understand the customer's perspective.
    - Apologize for the inconvenience and offer to help resolve the issue.
- An employee is struggling to meet their sales goals. A stoic retail manager would:
    - Talk to the employee about the challenges they are facing.
    - Offer them support and encouragement.
    - Help them develop a plan to improve their performance.
- A store is experiencing a sudden surge in customer traffic. A stoic retail manager would:
    - Remain calm and assess the situation
    - Involve employees in strategizing a resolution and an action plan for dealing with the situation.
    - Delegate tasks to their employees.
    - Communicate effectively with customers to keep them informed.

Retail managers can handle challenging situations with grace and composure if they follow Stoic ideals. They can also have a better connection with their staff and customers, which can lead to a more pleasant environment at the workplace.

Stoicism is a powerful philosophy that may be applied to many aspects of life, including retail management. Retail managers can minimize stress, improve decision-making, increase productivity, and lead with empathy by following stoic principles. These advantages can lead to a more successful and enjoyable career in retail.

Chapter 5

Stoicism in Middle Management

*T*he often-overlooked backbone of organizations, middle managers, play a critical role in corporate success. They serve as a link between top-level executives and front-line employees, translating strategic visions into actionable plans and ensuring that initiatives are carried out successfully. Their ability to inspire, coach, and develop their teams is critical for increasing productivity, innovation, and customer satisfaction.

Middle managers are responsible for aligning their teams with the overall goals and objectives of the organization. They deconstruct high-level strategies into concrete tasks and clearly communicate them to their employees. They also keep track of progress, identify roadblocks, and make adjustments as needed to keep initiatives on track.

Middle managers act as conduits of information, ensuring that communication flows seamlessly between top-level executives and frontline employees. They interpret and relay strategic decisions to their teams, while also gathering feedback and concerns from the ground level. This two-way communication fosters understanding, collaboration, and a sense of shared purpose.

Middle managers are critical in attracting, developing, and retaining top talent. They provide opportunities for growth, mentorship, and professional development to their employees. They also foster an atmosphere in which employees feel valued, respected, and encouraged to share their ideas.

Middle managers are frequently at the forefront of innovation, encouraging their teams to think creatively and try out new ideas. They also serve as change agents for their organizations, assisting them in adapting to new technologies, market trends, and competitive pressures.

Employee morale and engagement are directly influenced by middle managers. They foster a positive and supportive work environment in which employees feel valued, recognized, and rewarded for their efforts. They also respond to employee concerns quickly and effectively, fostering trust and loyalty.

Essential Qualities for Middle Managers

In today's dynamic business environment, characterized by rapid change and uncertainty, stoicism offers middle managers a powerful framework for developing the essential qualities of proactive management and adaptability. Stoicism's emphasis on reason, virtue, and accepting what is beyond our control can empower middle managers to navigate challenges with composure, make rational decisions, and seize new opportunities amidst uncertainty.

A stoic middle manager takes a proactive approach to change, anticipating potential issues and addressing them before they become major issues. They gather information, identify trends, and develop contingency plans to mitigate potential disruptions, guided by logic and analysis. This proactive approach enables them to stay ahead of the curve, minimizing the impact of change and ensuring the productivity and resilience of their teams.

Another characteristic of a stoic middle manager is adaptability, or the ability to navigate change and seize new opportunities effectively. They remain calm and composed in the face of change, drawing on Stoic principles and understanding that some things are beyond their control. Instead of dwelling on uncertainties, they direct their attention to what they can control, adapting their strategies and approaches to match with new realities.

Stoicism provides a solid foundation for proactive and adaptable leadership, empowering middle managers to navigate the complexities of today's business environment. By embracing stoic principles, middle managers can cultivate the resilience, rational decision-making, and adaptability needed to lead their teams effectively through periods of change and uncertainty. In doing so, they foster a thriving work environment where innovation, growth, and success can flourish.

Proactive managers are not merely reactive to problems; they are constantly scanning the horizon for potential risks and opportunities. They gather information, analyze trends, and develop contingency plans to mitigate potential disruptions. By taking a proactive approach, middle managers can:

- Prevent problems from escalating: By identifying and addressing potential issues early on, managers can prevent them from becoming major crises. This saves time, resources, and reputational damage.

- Maximize opportunities: Proactive managers are always looking for new ways to improve their teams and organizations. They are open to new ideas and willing to experiment with new approaches.

- Foster a culture of resilience: By anticipating and preparing for change, proactive managers create a sense of stability and confidence among their teams. This helps organizations weather storms and emerge stronger.

The ability to adapt to change is important for middle managers in today's rapidly evolving business landscape. It is also an important feature of stoicism. Adaptable managers are comfortable with uncertainty, can learn new things quickly, and are open to new ways of working. They can:

- Effectively implement new strategies: Adaptable managers can understand and implement new strategies without being paralyzed by the fear of change. They are able to communicate change effectively and help their teams embrace new ways of working.

- Respond to market disruptions: Adaptable managers can assess the impact of market disruptions and develop strategies to adapt to new realities. They can help their teams pivot and find new opportunities in the midst of change.

- Embrace continuous improvement: Adaptable managers are always looking for ways to improve their teams and organizations. They are open to feedback and willing to experiment with new approaches.

Organizations can cultivate proactive and adaptable middle managers by:

- Providing training and development opportunities: Offer workshops, seminars, and coaching programs that teach proactive problem-solving, change management, and adaptability skills.
- Encouraging a culture of learning and innovation: Foster an environment where employees are encouraged to think critically, ask questions, and experiment with new ideas.
- Empowering middle managers to take risks: Give middle managers the autonomy and resources they need to experiment with new approaches and take calculated risks.
- Recognizing and rewarding proactive and adaptable behavior: Celebrate successes and provide incentives for

employees who demonstrate proactive problem-solving and adaptability.

Proactive management and adaptability are essential qualities for middle managers in today's dynamic business environment. By developing these skills, middle managers can play a pivotal role in driving organizational success. Organizations that invest in cultivating proactive and adaptable middle managers are well-positioned to thrive in the face of change and uncertainty.

Leading Teams to Meet Targets and KPIs

Middle managers play an important role in leading their teams to meet targets and KPIs. By setting clear expectations, providing regular feedback, and offering support and encouragement, middle managers can help their teams achieve their goals.

The first step to leading teams to meet targets and KPIs is to set clear expectations. This means clearly defining the goals and objectives that the team is expected to achieve. Expectations should be realistic, measurable, and achievable. They should also be aligned with the overall goals of the organization.

Once expectations have been set, it is important to communicate them clearly to the team. This can be done through a variety of channels, such as team meetings, one-on-one conversations, and written documentation. It is also important to make sure that the team understands the rationale behind the expectations.

Regular feedback is essential for helping teams meet targets and KPIs. Feedback should be specific, timely, and actionable. It should also be focused on both positive and negative performance.

Positive feedback can help to motivate and encourage team members. It can also help to reinforce good behavior. Negative feedback should be delivered constructively and should focus on areas where the individual or team can improve.

It is also important to provide regular feedback on progress toward targets and KPIs. This helps to keep the team on track and identify any potential roadblocks.

Middle managers should provide their teams with the support and encouragement they need to succeed. This includes providing access to resources, training, and development opportunities. It also means creating a positive and supportive work environment.

Middle managers should also be willing to offer help and guidance when needed. This can include providing advice on how to overcome challenges, offering suggestions for improvement, and helping to troubleshoot problems.

Stoicism is a philosophy that emphasizes virtue, reason, and accepting what is beyond our control. It can be a valuable tool for middle managers who are leading their teams to meet targets and KPIs.

Stoic principles can help middle managers to:

- Remain calm and focused under pressure. This can be helpful when dealing with setbacks or challenges.
- Make decisions based on reason and evidence. This can help to avoid impulsive or emotional decisions.
- Accept that some things are beyond our control. This can help to reduce stress and anxiety.

In addition, stoicism can help middle managers to develop the following qualities that are essential for effective leadership:

- Courage: The ability to face challenges and take risks.
- Resilience: The ability to bounce back from setbacks.
- Fairness: The ability to treat others with respect and justice.
- Humility: The ability to admit mistakes and learn from them.

Leading teams to meet targets and KPIs is a challenging task. However, by setting clear expectations, providing regular feedback, and offering support and encouragement, middle managers can help their teams achieve their goals. Stoicism can be a valuable tool for middle managers who are leading their teams to success. By cultivating stoic virtues such as courage, resilience, fairness, and humility, middle managers can create a positive and productive work environment where their teams can thrive.

A stoic middle manager is not merely a passive observer of events but an active agent of change, guided by reason and virtue. They embody a steadfast character, remaining calm and composed in the face of adversity, while making rational decisions and inspiring their teams with unwavering determination.

Key Characteristics of a Stoic Middle Manager

1. **Emotional Discipline:** They possess the ability to manage their emotions effectively, preventing impulsive reactions and maintaining composure under pressure.
2. **Rational Decision-Making:** They base their decisions on logic, evidence, and careful consideration, avoiding impulsive or emotional choices.
3. **Acceptance and Adaptability:** They accept that some things are beyond their control and focus their energy on

what they can influence, adapting to changing circumstances with grace and resilience.

4. **Focus on the Present:** They maintain a present-minded focus, avoiding dwelling on past regrets or worrying about future uncertainties.

5. **Continuous Learning and Growth:** They embrace continuous learning and self-improvement, actively seeking opportunities to expand their knowledge and skills.

6. **Fairness and Impartiality:** They treat all team members with respect and fairness, avoiding favoritism and upholding a sense of justice.

7. **Humility and Self-Awareness:** They recognize their own limitations and are open to learning from others including members of their own teams.

Examples of Stoicism in Action

1. Navigating Change with Serenity: A stoic middle manager, faced with a sudden organizational restructuring, remains calm and composed, explaining the changes to their team in a clear and rational manner. They acknowledge the challenges but emphasize the opportunities for growth and development.

2. Turning Setbacks into Learning Opportunities: A stoic middle manager, confronted with a failed product launch, gathers their team to analyze the situation. They encourage open and honest discussions, focusing on identifying lessons learned and strategies for improvement.

3. Motivating Through Resilience: A stoic middle manager, leading a team through a period of financial hardship, exudes unwavering optimism and determination. They inspire their team by demonstrating unwavering belief in their capabilities and emphasizing the importance of perseverance.

4. Empowering Through Trust: A stoic middle manager, fostering a culture of autonomy and trust, empowers their team members to take ownership of their work. They provide guidance and support while encouraging independent decision-making.

5. Cultivating a Growth Mindset: A stoic middle manager, recognizing the importance of continuous learning, encourages their team to embrace challenges as opportunities for growth. They foster a culture of open communication, where feedback is valued and mistakes are seen as stepping stones to improvement.

6. Facing Unforeseen Challenges with Resolve: A stoic middle manager, dealing with an unexpected crisis, remains calm and focused. They quickly assess the situation, develop a contingency plan, and communicate it clearly to their team. They inspire confidence and determination, guiding their team through the challenges.

In the ever-evolving landscape of business, stoicism offers middle managers a powerful framework for effective leadership. By embracing stoic principles, middle managers can cultivate resilience, inspire their teams with unwavering determination, and foster a thriving work environment where growth and success are within reach.

The following situational examples illustrate how a stoic middle manager's reaction would differentiate from a middle manager who is not stoic, with more detailed descriptions:

Situation 1:

A key team member resigns unexpectedly.

Non-Stoic Middle Manager:

- Reacts impulsively and emotionally, expressing anger or frustration. "How could they do this to us now?", they exclaim, feeling betrayed and abandoned.
- Blames the departing team member or other factors for the situation. "They were never really committed to the team," they conclude, failing to acknowledge any potential contributing factors within the organization.
- Scrambles to find a replacement without a clear plan or strategy. They rush into hiring the first available candidate without considering the team's needs and the long-term impact.

Stoic Middle Manager:

- Remains calm and composed, acknowledging the loss but not dwelling on it. They understand that people leave for various reasons and that it's important to focus on moving forward.
- Analyzes the reasons for the team member's departure and identifies potential areas for improvement. They gather feedback from colleagues and conduct a thorough review of the team's dynamics to identify any underlying issues.
- Develops a structured plan to find a replacement, considering both internal and external candidates. They

create a detailed job description, outline the recruitment process, and involve key stakeholders in the decision-making.

Situation 2:

A critical project faces unexpected delays and setbacks.

Non-Stoic Middle Manager:

- Panics and micromanages the team, creating a stressful and unproductive environment. They constantly hover over team members, demanding updates and making impulsive decisions without consulting the team.
- Places blame on individuals or external factors rather than seeking solutions. They point fingers at specific team members or external circumstances, failing to take responsibility for overall project management.
- Loses sight of the overall objectives and becomes overwhelmed by the challenges. They get bogged down in the immediate problems, losing focus on the project's goals and priorities.

Stoic Middle Manager:

- Maintains composure and focuses on identifying the root causes of the delays. They calmly gather information, analyze data, and seek input from team members to understand the underlying issues.
- Collaborates with the team to develop strategies for overcoming the challenges. They involve the team in brainstorming solutions, considering their expertise and perspectives.
- Reassesses the project timeline and adjusts expectations accordingly. They communicate the revised timeline clearly and transparently to all stakeholders, ensuring everyone is on the same page.

Situation 3:

A customer complaint escalates into a public relations crisis.

Non-Stoic Middle Manager:

- Reacts defensively and attempts to deflect responsibility for the situation. They become aggressive and argumentative, refusing to acknowledge any shortcomings on their part.

- Engages in a public war of words with the customer, further escalating the conflict. They respond to customer complaints with hostility and sarcasm, fueling the negative publicity.
- Fails to take ownership of the problem and address the customer's concerns promptly. They delay addressing the issue, allowing the situation to spiral out of control and damage the company's reputation.

Stoic Middle Manager:

- Acknowledges the customer's concerns and apologizes for any inconvenience caused. They take responsibility for the situation, demonstrating empathy and a willingness to make things right.
- Takes ownership of the problem and initiates a thorough investigation to identify the root cause. They gather all relevant information, analyze customer feedback, and involve relevant departments to address the issue.
- Communicates transparently with the customer and stakeholders, outlining steps to resolve the issue. They provide regular updates, keep stakeholders informed, and address customer concerns promptly and effectively.

Situation 4:

A team member repeatedly misses deadlines and fails to meet performance expectations.

Non-Stoic Middle Manager:

- Reacts with anger or frustration, creating a hostile and unproductive work environment. They lash out at the team member, making personal attacks and undermining their morale.
- Publicly reprimands the team member, damaging their confidence and reputation. They criticize the team member in front of colleagues, further embarrassing and discouraging them.
- Fails to provide constructive feedback and guidance to help the team member improve. They offer vague or unhelpful feedback, failing to identify specific areas for improvement or provide actionable steps.

Stoic Middle Manager:

- Engages in a private conversation with the team member to understand the underlying reasons for their performance issues. They listen actively and empathetically, seeking to understand the challenges the team member is facing.

- Provides constructive feedback and identifies areas for improvement, offering support and resources. They focus on specific behaviors or performance gaps, offering concrete suggestions and resources for improvement.
- Develops a performance improvement plan and regularly monitors progress. They set clear expectations, establish milestones, and provide regular feedback to track the team member's progress and provide ongoing support.

Situation 5:

A company undergoes a significant restructuring, resulting in layoffs and organizational changes.

Non-Stoic Middle Manager:

- Spreads negativity and uncertainty among their team, undermining morale and productivity. They openly express their own anxieties and fears, creating a sense of panic and instability within the team.
- Expresses personal concerns about the restructuring rather than focusing on supporting the team. They prioritize their own job security and advancement

opportunities, failing to provide the necessary support and guidance to their team members during this difficult time.

- Fails to provide clear communication and guidance to team members during the transition. They avoid addressing difficult questions or providing clear information about the restructuring, leaving team members feeling lost and uncertain.

Stoic Middle Manager:

- Remains calm and composed, acknowledging the challenges while emphasizing the opportunities for growth. They understand that change can be difficult but also presents opportunities for new beginnings and personal development.

- Provides regular updates and transparent communication to the team, addressing their concerns and uncertainties. They hold regular meetings, distribute written updates, and make themselves available for individual discussions to address team members' questions and concerns.

- Focuses on supporting team members through the transition, offering guidance and assistance in finding new opportunities. They provide outplacement services, connect team members with relevant networks, and offer career counseling to assist team members in their job search.

By embracing stoic principles, middle managers can cultivate resilience, inspire their teams with unwavering determination, and foster a thriving work environment where growth and success are within reach.

Studies have shown that companies with strong middle management teams tend to outperform those with weak teams. Effective middle managers are associated with a number of positive outcomes, including:

- Increased employee productivity and engagement
- Improved customer satisfaction and loyalty
- Enhanced innovation and adaptability
- Reduced turnover and absenteeism
- Stronger corporate financial performance

Given the critical role they play in corporate success, organizations should invest in the development and training of their middle managers. This includes providing them with opportunities to attend leadership workshops, conferences, and other professional development programs. It also means giving them the resources and autonomy they need to do their jobs effectively.

Middle managers are the unsung heroes of corporate success. They are the glue that holds organizations together, translating visions into reality and driving performance. By investing in their development and empowering them to succeed, organizations can reap significant rewards in terms of employee satisfaction, innovation, and financial growth.

Chapter 6

Stoicism in Sr. Leadership

Senior leaders have a plethora of challenges and obligations in today's dynamic and ever-changing business market. They are responsible for navigating their organizations through challenging times, making important decisions that shape their future, and inspiring their people to reach lofty goals. Amidst this demanding environment, stoicism emerges as a powerful framework for effective senior leadership.

Stoicism, an ancient philosophy emphasizing virtue, reason, and acceptance of what is beyond our control, offers a set of principles that can empower senior leaders to navigate challenges with composure, make rational decisions, and inspire their teams to achieve excellence. By embracing stoicism, senior leaders can cultivate the resilience, wisdom, and determination needed to steer their organizations towards success.

Stoic leadership is defined by a distinct mindset that includes emotional resilience, rational decision-making, acceptance and flexibility, a growth mindset, and humility. Stoic leaders are able to remain calm and composed in the face of hardship, make accurate choices based on evidence, welcome change with flexibility, seek for constant growth, and acknowledge their own limitations.

Stoic leaders develop emotional resilience by acknowledging and accepting their emotions without allowing them to control them. They know how feelings can impair judgment and make it difficult to make efficient decisions. They use emotional regulation techniques such as mindfulness and self-reflection to maintain composure and focus in the face of adversity, rather than reacting impulsively.

Their ability to effectively manage their emotions sets a good example for their teams, demonstrating that it is possible to remain calm, collected, and focused on finding solutions even in difficult situations. This calm promotes a sense of stability and confidence within the organization, allowing team members to approach challenges with the same emotional resilience.

Stoic leaders make decisions based on logic and evidence, avoiding rash or emotional decisions. They gather information, analyze data, and consult with experts before making decisions to gain a comprehensive understanding of the situation. This approach ensures that their decisions are well-informed, strategic, and in line with the overall goals of the organization.

Stoic leaders stand out in a world where quick decisions are frequently regarded as a sign of leadership for their ability to take a step back, carefully consider all available information, and make decisions based on sound reasoning and analysis. This approach instills trust in their team members, who understand that their decisions are based on a thorough understanding of the situation at hand rather than gut instincts or hasty reactions.

Stoic leaders recognize that change is unavoidable and that some things are out of their hands. They embrace change as an opportunity for growth and learning rather than resisting or fearing it. They modify their strategies and approaches as needed, remaining adaptable and resourceful in the face of changing conditions.

Accepting change does not imply resignation or passivity; rather, it means acknowledging that some things are beyond our control and focusing our efforts on what we can influence. Stoic leaders demonstrate this principle by proactively anticipating potential changes, developing contingency plans, and guiding their teams through transitions with composure and adaptability.

Stoic leaders embody a growth mindset, believing that their abilities can be developed through effort and learning. They actively seek feedback, practice continuous learning, and view challenges as opportunities to broaden their knowledge and skills. This mindset fosters an innovative culture and encourages team members to push their limits.

By demonstrating a commitment to personal growth, stoic leaders inspire their teams to adopt a similar mindset. They actively seek feedback, practice continuous learning, and view challenges as opportunities to broaden their knowledge and skills. This mindset fosters an innovative culture and encourages team members to constructively push their limits.

Stoic leaders are self-aware and humble, acknowledging their own limitations and seeking feedback from others. They are open to learning from their mistakes, admitting their flaws, and seeking expert advice when necessary. This openness to feedback promotes a transparent culture and encourages team members to share their ideas and concerns without fear of being judged.

In a world where many leaders are under pressure to project an image of invincibility, stoic leaders stand out for their willingness to admit their flaws and seek feedback from others. This humility demonstrates respect for the team's collective wisdom and fosters an environment conducive to open communication and collaboration.

The principles of stoicism can be effectively applied in various aspects of senior leadership practices, enabling leaders to navigate complex situations, make sound decisions, and inspire their teams towards excellence.

Visionary Leadership

Setting a Clear and Stoic-Grounded Vision

Stoic leaders set clear and inspiring visions for their organizations, grounded in stoic principles. They communicate this vision with clarity and conviction, ensuring that all stakeholders understand the direction the organization is heading and the values that underpin it. Their stoic approach inspires team members and motivates them to align their efforts with the overall vision.

A stoic-grounded vision is about articulating a clear and compelling sense of purpose that resonates with the organization's mission, values, and stakeholders, rather than making grand pronouncements or making unrealistic promises. It is about developing a common understanding of the organization's goals and the steps required to achieve them.

Leaders can inspire confidence and foster a sense of unity among team members by anchoring their vision in stoic principles, even in the face of challenges and uncertainties. This shared vision serves as a guiding light, inspiring individuals to give their all-in order to achieve common goals.

Strategic Decision-Making

Navigating Complex Choices with Rational Analysis

When faced with complex decisions, stoic leaders employ rational analysis and evidence-based reasoning. They gather information, consider multiple points of view, and carefully weigh the implications of each option. This approach ensures that their decisions are well-informed, strategic, and aligned with the long-term goals of the organization.

In the fast-paced and often data-driven world of business, it is easy to make rash decisions based on limited information or gut feelings. Stoic leaders, on the other hand, resist this temptation and carefully weigh all factors before making a decision.

Stoic leaders use rational analysis and evidence-based reasoning to make decisions that are not only sound but also defendable. This approach fosters trust among team members and stakeholders, who understand that their leaders are making informed decisions that are in line with the organization's goals.

Crisis Management

Leading Through Adversity with Calmness and Resilience

Stoic leaders remain calm and composed in times of crisis, providing stability and reassurance to their teams. They rationally assess the situation, devise contingency plans, and communicate clearly with stakeholders. Their stoic demeanor inspires confidence and encourages team members to collaborate effectively in navigating the challenges.

Crisis management is an important aspect of senior leadership that necessitates the ability to remain calm and collected under pressure, make quick and informed decisions, and effectively communicate with a wide range of stakeholders. Stoic principles lay a strong foundation for crisis leadership, allowing leaders to navigate difficult situations with calmness and resilience.

By demonstrating calmness and composure in the face of adversity, stoic leaders set an example for their teams, fostering a sense of stability and confidence during times of uncertainty. This approach allows the organization to focus on addressing the crisis effectively and emerge from it stronger and more resilient.

Stakeholder Management

Building Trust and Maintaining Relationships

Stoic leaders cultivate strong relationships with key stakeholders, fostering trust and understanding. They approach stakeholder interactions with empathy, transparency, and a willingness to listen to different perspectives. This strategy fosters goodwill, fortifies alliances, and enhances the organization's reputation.

In today's interconnected business world, effective stakeholder management is critical for long-term success. Stoic principles provide a framework for building strong, long-term relationships with key stakeholders, ensuring that their interests are considered and communication channels are kept open.

Stoic leaders establish trust with stakeholders by demonstrating empathy, transparency, and a willingness to listen. This lays the groundwork for mutually beneficial relationships. This approach not only enhances the organization's reputation but also strengthens its ability to navigate challenges and seize opportunities.

Team Empowerment

Creating an Environment Where Team Members Thrive

Stoic leaders foster an environment in which team members feel valued, empowered, and encouraged to give their all. They provide clear direction, support and mentorship, and recognize individual and team accomplishments. This approach encourages team members to feel a sense of ownership, engagement, and innovation.

Empowering teams does not mean abdicating responsibility; rather, it means creating an environment in which people feel valued, trusted, and encouraged to take ownership of their work.

Stoic leaders cultivate this environment by providing clear direction, offering support and mentorship, and celebrating successes.

Stoic leaders unleash the collective potential of their organizations by empowering their teams, allowing individuals to contribute their unique talents and perspectives to achieving common goals. This approach results in increased innovation, productivity, and engagement, thereby setting the stage for long term success.

Case Studies of Stoic Senior Leaders

Throughout history, numerous stoic leaders have demonstrated the effectiveness of stoic principles in guiding organizations through challenging times and achieving remarkable success. By examining their leadership styles, decisions, and impact, we can gain valuable insights into the practical application of stoicism in senior leadership.

George Washington was the United States' first president. He is remembered for his honesty, integrity, and calm demeanor under pressure. He led the Continental Army to victory in the American Revolutionary War and was instrumental in shaping the new nation. His stoic leadership style helped to establish democratic and self-government principles in the United States.

Nelson Mandela is an anti-apartheid revolutionary, political leader, and philanthropist known for his courage, tenacity, and commitment to justice. He spent 27 years in prison for his anti-apartheid activism, but he came out with a firm belief in the power of forgiveness and reconciliation. He exemplified the Stoic virtues of wisdom, courage, and justice during South Africa's democratic transition.

Jack Dorsey is X's (formerly Twitter) co-founder and former CEO who is well known for his emphasis on transparency, open communication, and self-reflection. To navigate the challenges of leading a rapidly growing tech company while remaining committed to its core values, he adopted Stoic principles.

Mark Zuckerberg, Meta (formerly Facebook) co-founder and CEO known for his vision, determination, and adaptability in changing circumstances. He has drawn inspiration from Stoic philosophy in his approach to leadership, emphasizing the importance of rational decision-making, emotional resilience, and a long-term perspective.

Sheryl Sandberg is Meta's COO and is well-known for her strategic thinking, collaborative approach, and commitment to empowering women in leadership. She has incorporated Stoic principles into her leadership style, emphasizing the importance of clear communication, effective emotion management, and making decisions based on evidence and analysis.

These examples demonstrate that stoicism remains a relevant and valuable framework for senior leadership in the modern world. By embodying stoic principles, senior leaders can more successfully navigate complex challenges, make sound decisions, and inspire their teams to achieve excellence.

By examining the leadership styles, decisions, and impact of these stoic figures, we can identify common themes and principles that underpin their effectiveness.

Composure and Rationality amid hardship: Stoic leaders are known for their exceptional composure and rationality in the face of hardship. Instead of reacting impulsively or emotionally, they remain calm under pressure, thoroughly analyze their choices, and make judgments based on reason and evidence.

Commitment to Virtue and Ethical Leadership: Strong moral values guide Stoic leaders, emphasizing honesty, integrity, fairness, and justice. They set a good example by exhibiting the qualities they expect from their teams and upholding ethical standards in all of their decisions and activities.

Focus on Long-Term aims and Impact: Stoic leaders keep a long-term perspective, making decisions that line with the organization's overarching aims and ideals. They eschew short-term thinking and prioritize measures that will benefit the organization's future.

Adaptability and Acceptance of Change: Stoic leaders know that change is unavoidable and adjust their plans and approaches accordingly. They stay open to new ideas and are eager to welcome change as an opportunity for growth and creativity.

Emphasis on Self-Reflection and Continuous Improvement: Stoic leaders are committed to self-reflection and continuous improvement. They seek feedback, acknowledge their shortcomings, and actively work to develop their leadership skills and knowledge.

These common themes highlight the transformative power of stoicism in shaping effective senior leadership. By embracing stoic principles, leaders can cultivate the resilience, wisdom, and determination needed to steer their organizations towards success in an increasingly complex and challenging world.

Stoicism offers a timeless and powerful framework for effective senior leadership. By embodying stoic principles, leaders can cultivate the resilience, wisdom, and determination needed to guide their organizations through turbulent times, make sound decisions, and inspire their teams to achieve excellence.

Stoicism is a significant source of direction for senior leaders as we negotiate the ever-changing terrain of the modern world. Leaders may empower themselves and their teams to overcome problems, grasp opportunities, and leave a lasting beneficial impact on the world by embracing its values of composure, logic, virtue, and adaptability.

The following five situational examples illustrate how a stoic senior leader's reaction in a corporate setting would differentiate from any other senior leadership who is not stoic, with more detailed descriptions:

Situation 1:

A sudden market downturn causes significant financial losses for the company.

Non-Stoic Senior Leader:

- May react with panic and blames external factors for the situation. They may lash out at subordinates, make impulsive decisions, and project an image of fear and uncertainty.

- May prioritize immediate cost-cutting measures without considering the long-term impact on the company's growth and innovation potential.
- Fails to communicate effectively with employees, leading to anxiety, confusion, and a decline in morale.

Stoic Senior Leader:

- Remains calm and composed, acknowledging the challenges while emphasizing the company's resilience and adaptability.
- Gathers information, analyzes the situation thoroughly, and involves key stakeholders in developing a response plan.
- Prioritizes the well-being of employees, providing clear communication, support, and reassurance during challenging times.

Situation 2:

A key employee resigns abruptly, leaving a critical project without leadership.

Non-Stoic Senior Leader:

- Reacts with anger and frustration, placing blame on the departing employee and questioning their loyalty.
- Rushes to fill the vacancy without carefully considering the qualifications and experience of potential replacements.
- Fails to address the underlying reasons for the employee's departure, potentially leading to further resignations and a decline in employee morale.

Stoic Senior Leader:

- Maintains composure and focuses on ensuring the project's continuation.
- Analyzes the reasons for the employee's departure and identifies potential areas for improvement within the organization.
- Develops a structured plan to find a replacement, considering both internal and external candidates.

Situation 3:

A customer expresses dissatisfaction with a product or service, leading to negative media coverage.

Non-Stoic Senior Leader:

- May react defensively and attempts to deflect responsibility for the situation. They may engage in a public war of words with the customer, further escalating the conflict.
- Fails to take ownership of the problem and address the customer's concerns promptly and effectively.
- Allows the negative media coverage to damage the company's reputation and customer loyalty.

Stoic Senior Leader:

- Acknowledges the customer's concerns and apologizes for any inconvenience caused. They take responsibility for the situation and initiate a thorough investigation to identify the root cause.
- Communicates transparently with the customer and stakeholders, outlining steps to resolve the issue.
- Addresses the underlying problems to prevent similar incidents from recurring.

Situation 4:

The company faces a significant ethical dilemma involving a potential business partner.

Non-Stoic Senior Leader:

- May prioritize short-term gains over ethical considerations, compromising the company's values and reputation.
- May make impulsive decisions based on personal biases or fear of missing out on opportunities.
- Fails to seek diverse perspectives and consider the long-term implications of the ethical dilemma.

Stoic Senior Leader:

- Gathers all relevant information, analyzes the situation from various ethical frameworks, and involves key stakeholders in the decision-making process.
- Prioritizes upholding the company's ethical standards, even if it means sacrificing potential short-term gains.
- Communicates the decision clearly and transparently, maintaining a strong ethical compass.

Situation 5:

The company undergoes a significant restructuring, resulting in layoffs and organizational changes.

Non-Stoic Senior Leader:

- May prioritize their own job security and advancement opportunities, failing to provide adequate support and guidance to affected employees.
- May communicate the restructuring in a vague or insensitive manner, leading to anxiety, confusion, and a decline in morale.
- Fails to provide clear transition plans and outplacement services for laid-off employees.

Stoic Senior Leader:

- Remains calm and supportive, acknowledging the challenges and providing reassurance to affected employees.
- Communicates the restructuring with transparency and empathy, addressing concerns and questions openly.
- Provides outplacement services, connects affected employees with relevant networks, and offers career counseling to assist them in their job search.

Chapter 7

Executive Stoics

*N*ow, let's talk about using stoicism when you're a big leader – like a CEO or a top executive. These leaders have a bunch of tough jobs. They steer the ship, make big decisions, and inspire everyone around them. In this busy world, stoicism becomes like a secret weapon for these leaders.

Imagine a boss who seems like a superhero of decision-making. This superhero isn't just about making choices; they're also great at steering their team through all kinds of tricky situations. Let's call them the "Executive Stoic."

Executive Stoics are the cool, calm, and collected leaders in a company. Imagine your boss handling challenges without breaking a sweat – that's them! These leaders don't just make decisions;

they make superhero-level decisions that affect everyone in the company.

Now, these Executive Stoics have a bag full of tricks. They navigate the difficult parts of their job with wisdom, which is like having a superpower in the business world. When things get tough, they don't lose their cool; instead, they stay calm and composed, like a superhero facing challenges without breaking a sweat.

But what sets them apart is not just their wisdom and composure; it's their superhero code. This code is all about doing the right thing, being fair, and making choices that are good not just for them but for everyone in the team. It's like having a moral compass that always points towards what's good and fair.

Now, being an Executive Stoic means dealing with lots of challenges. It's like going through a tricky maze every day. But guess what? These leaders smile in the face of challenges. They know that being cool and collected is their superpower. When things get crazy, they don't panic; they think wisely and act calmly.

Imagine having a crystal ball that shows the future. Well, Executive Stoics have something like that – it's called a "long-term perspective." Instead of just looking at what's happening now, they peek into the future. This helps them make choices that might be tough today but fantastic for the team's success tomorrow.

Now, every superhero needs a superpower, right? For Executive Stoics, it's resilience. When something doesn't go as planned, they bounce back. It's like they have a rubber ball inside them – no matter how hard it gets thrown, they come back stronger. This resilience is like the secret sauce that keeps their team going, no matter what.

So, what does it mean to be an "Executive Stoic"? It's about having a special way of thinking. Picture this: you stay cool when things get tough, make smart choices based on facts, and don't let what you can't change overwhelm you. That's the stoic way for executive leaders.

Executive Stoics keep calm even when everything goes crazy. They don't let emotions take over. Instead, they use tricks like mindfulness to stay focused. By doing this, they set an example for their team, showing it's possible to face problems without losing your cool.

These leaders don't just roll dice to decide things. Nope, they gather facts, talk to experts, and really dig into info before making choices. This makes their decisions strong and smart. While many leaders rush, Executive Stoics take their time, making sure they're on the right path.

Change is part of life, and Executive Stoics know it. Instead of fighting it, they see change as a chance to learn and grow. They adjust plans, stay flexible, and don't stress over things they can't control. This helps them lead through the twists and turns of the business world.

Executive Stoics believe they can get better every day. They ask for feedback, learn new stuff, and see challenges as chances to shine. This "always learning" idea spreads to their team, creating a group of people hungry to grow and improve.

These leaders aren't about breathing up their chests. Nope, they know they're not perfect. Executive Stoics admit when they mess up, ask for advice, and don't act like they know it all. This humble vibe makes their teams feel safe to speak up and share ideas.

Let's see how this stoic stuff works in the big-league tasks of executive roles.

Executive Stoics make sure everyone knows where the ship is sailing. They share a clear vision, making sure everyone gets why they're doing what they're doing. It's not about big speeches; it's about making sure everyone's on the same page, working towards the same goals.

Executive Stoics don't let stress and problems get to them. They stay calm even when everything seems like it's falling apart. Instead of getting overwhelmed by emotions, they use tricks like mindfulness to stay focused. This not only helps them but sets a good example for their team, showing that challenges can be faced without losing your cool.

Connecting with people is a big deal for Executive Stoics. They build strong relationships with everyone involved – from employees to partners. By being open, understanding, and really listening, they create a network of trust that helps the company thrive.

Executive Stoics don't lead with an iron fist. They create a space where everyone feels valued and ready to give their best. By giving clear directions, supporting their team, and celebrating wins, they bring out the best in everyone.

Executives are like decision-making wizards. They make calls that influence the whole company, from what projects to invest in to who leads different teams. Their decisions shape the company's path. Each decision, big or small, has a ripple effect on every employee.

Now, making decisions is only part of the task. The other important part is letting everyone know about these decisions.

Picture it as the captain announcing the course changes to the crew. A smart executive knows that just making a decision isn't enough; they need to communicate it clearly.

How you say things matters as much as what you say. An executive's words are like the wind guiding the ship. If they communicate decisions well, everyone understands where the company is heading. But if they mumble or speak in confusing terms, it's like sailing into a storm without a compass.

Now, the special ingredient here is being a "stoic" executive. These leaders make tough decisions – the ones that aren't easy but necessary. Then, they step up and take responsibility. They don't hide behind closed doors; they face the crew (employees) and explain the changes.

Imagine the captain saying, "We're changing course because it's the best way to reach our destination safely." That's what the stoic executive does. They say, "We're making these changes for the good of the company, and I take responsibility for them." This honesty and openness builds trust among the crew.

A stoic executive doesn't just throw decisions at the crew. They connect those decisions to the values and integrity of the company. If a decision is about focusing on quality, they explain, "This move is to keep our promise of delivering top-notch products." It's like showing the map and explaining why this new route is the best one.

By communicating decisions with clarity, values, and integrity, stoic executives ensure a smooth sail for the company. The crew understands where they're going, why, and how each person plays a role. This creates a united crew, ready to face any storm because they trust their captain.

Here's the cool part: when the crew trusts the captain, they work better together. When decisions are communicated well, everyone is on the same page, rowing in the same direction. This unity is like a domino effect, making the company more efficient and resilient.

Stoic executives don't just handle smooth seas. They shine in stormy weather too. When a decision is especially tough, they don't shy away. Instead, they communicate even more clearly. It's like saying, "We're facing a storm, but here's our plan, and we'll get through it together."

In the end, being an executive is about steering the ship and guiding the crew. It's about making decisions, even the tough ones, and then being the voice that explains those decisions. A stoic executive understands that this communication is not just talking;

it's the heart of leadership, keeping the whole crew on course and ready for whatever the sea of business brings.

Looking at Real-Life Executive Stoics

The first U.S. president, George Washington, was a top-notch Executive Stoic. He stayed calm during the Revolutionary War, made smart choices, and set up the U.S. on the right path. His cool head and steady leadership shaped the country.

In more recent times, Nelson Mandela showed Executive Stoicism. Locked up for 27 years, he came out forgiving and ready to lead South Africa. His courage, justice, and wisdom guided the country through a big change.

Jumping to the present, leaders like Jack Dorsey (X) (Formerly Twitter), Mark Zuckerberg (Meta), and Sheryl Sandberg (Meta) use Stoic principled management approaches. From staying transparent to making smart decisions, they show how Executive Stoicism helps in today's fast-paced world.

These leaders show some cool moves that make them stand out:

- Keeping Calm: No matter what hits, they stay cool and focused.

- Choosing Ethical Paths: They make choices that match their company's values, even when it's tough.
- Thinking Long-Term: Instead of quick fixes, they plan for the future.

So, why should leaders care about this stoic stuff? Well, it's like a superpower. By being an Executive Stoic, leaders make more effective decisions, guide their teams through tough times, and create a workplace where everyone shines. It's like having a captain who not only knows how to sail through storms but also how to keep everyone on the ship together and motivated.

When a company has an Executive Stoic at the wheel, the whole team feels it. They work better together, trust each other more, and know they can face any challenge. It's like having a superhero leading the way, making sure everyone reaches success together.

Executive stoicism is not merely a set of theoretical concepts; it is a practical guide to leadership excellence. It encompasses a range of virtues and practices that empower leaders to navigate challenges, make sound decisions, and inspire their teams to achieve greatness with them.

At the heart of executive stoicism lie four fundamental characteristics:

Wisdom: The ability to discern truth from falsehood, make sound judgments, and act with prudence.

Courage: The strength to face challenges head-on, overcome adversity, and make difficult decisions with conviction.

Justice: The commitment to fairness, equity, and ethical conduct in all aspects of business.

Temperance: The ability to control one's emotions, impulses, and desires, fostering composure and rationality in the face of adversity.

These characteristics are not mere ideals; they are personal attributes cultivated through consistent practice. Here are some key stoic practices that can be adopted by executives:

Self-reflection: Regularly examine one's thoughts, actions, and motivations to identify areas for improvement and strengthen one's character.

Negative visualization: Envision potential obstacles and challenges that may arise, preparing mentally and emotionally to face them effectively.

Focus on the controllable: Direct energy and attention towards factors that can be influenced, rather than dwelling on those that cannot.

Acceptance of the uncontrollable: Recognize and accept that certain events are beyond one's control, fostering resilience and adaptability.

Memento mori: Regularly remind oneself of one's mortality, placing life's challenges in perspective and emphasizing the importance of living with purpose and integrity.

How can a Stoic Leader affect a Company and Organization's Culture and Work Environment?

A stoic leader can significantly impact an organization's work environment and culture. Here's how:

1. Stoic leaders foster a stable and tranquil environment because of their philosophical stance. They show resilience that can motivate the team by remaining calm in the face of

difficulty. This may result in a more deliberate, problem-solving-oriented, less reactive work atmosphere.

2. Overall stress levels in the workplace can be lowered by following these leaders' example and encouraging acceptance of circumstances beyond one's control. Workers might be less concerned about outside influences and more focused on their reactions and activities.

3. Since stoicism strongly emphasizes moral behavior, a stoic leader highly values honesty, fairness, and integrity. This dedication to morality can create a strong ethical culture within the company, encouraging respect and trust among staff members.

4. Emotionally intelligent, stoic leaders can keep a stable emotional state and empathize with the feelings of their team. This may foster a sympathetic and encouraging work atmosphere.

5. Leaders who practice stoicism tend to be less affected by temporary setbacks or difficulties because they maintain a long-term outlook and concentrate on the greater picture. This thinking can promote a growth mindset among team members, stimulate strategic thinking, and help the organization achieve long-term success.

Executive stoicism is not merely a theoretical concept; it is a practical guide to navigating the challenges of the corporate world. Let's consider some real-world situations and how a stoic approach would differ from a non-stoic one:

Situation 1:

A sudden market downturn causes significant financial losses for the company.

Non-stoic executive: Reacts with panic, blames external factors, and lashes out at subordinates, creating an environment of fear and uncertainty.

Stoic executive: Remains calm, acknowledges challenges, gathers information, analyzes the situation, and involves key stakeholders and team members in developing a response plan, prioritizing employee well-being and clear communication.

Situation 2:

A key employee abruptly resigns, leaving a critical project without leadership.

Non-stoic executive: Reacts with anger and frustration, placing blame on the departing employee, rushes to fill the vacancy without careful consideration, and fails to timely address underlying reasons for the departure. Concentrates on short-term resolution of problem.

Stoic executive: Maintains composure, analyzes reasons for the departure, identifies areas for improvement, develops a structured plan to find a replacement, and considers both internal and external candidates.

Situation 3:

A customer expresses dissatisfaction with a product or service, leading to negative media coverage.

Non-stoic executive: Reacts defensively, deflects responsibility, engages in a public war of words with the customer, escalates the conflict, fails to take ownership, and allows negative media to damage the company's reputation.

Stoic executive: Acknowledges customer concerns, apologizes, takes responsibility, initiates a thorough investigation, communicates transparently with stakeholders, outlines steps to resolve the issue from a longer term perspective, and addresses underlying problems to prevent recurrence.

Situation 4:

The company faces a significant ethical dilemma involving a potential business partner.

Non-stoic executive: May prioritize short-term gains over ethical considerations, compromising the company's values and reputation, make impulsive decisions based on personal biases, and fail to seek diverse perspectives.

Stoic executive: Gathers all relevant information, analyzes the situation from various ethical frameworks, involves key stakeholders and team members in the decision-making process, prioritizes upholding ethical standards, communicates the decision clearly and transparently, and maintains a strong ethical compass.

So, here's the big takeaway: Executive Stoics are like the Avengers of Wisdom. They handle challenges, make smart choices, and lead with a superhero code of fairness and integrity.

With their superpowers of composure, long-term vision, and resilience, they're not just bosses; they're the wise leaders who make their teams unstoppable.

Chapter 8

Stoic Business Owners

S toicism attracts from the foundation of good judgment and rationality. Stoicism also relies on a psychological aspect – one in which methods are used to project the onset of terrible thoughts like anger, anxiety, and grief.

The Stoics warned us to seek for peacefulness however reported that the world is filled with troubles to peace, which is mainly genuine when you're starting a business.

In an age where statistics and analysis rule; first, I inspire different tech business people to look beyond the numbers to increase an enterprise philosophy. Ask: what are the beliefs and values that power my business?

Business owners are often hit with a series of one-two gut punches daily, and often take them alone. In any given time, the company may be facing an economic decline, and the falling issues that follow. From managing employees and maintaining a constant positive cash flow to dealing with unexpected setbacks and making important decisions, running a small business can be overwhelming at times. One philosophy that can help small business owners make effective decisions and navigate these challenges is **stoicism**.

As a business owner, there will be many things that are outside of your control. This could include market conditions, the actions of your competitors, or even the behavior of your employees. Rather than stressing out or getting frustrated over these things, try to accept them as they are and focus on what you can control.

The Stoics believed that individuals have complete control over their own thoughts and actions. As a business owner, this means that you have the power to control how you respond to challenges and obstacles. By focusing on what you can control and taking action to improve your situation, you can become a more effective and successful manager/owner.

The special group in the business world – the Stoic Business Owners. These are the people steering their own ships, making decisions that shape their company's destiny. Being a business owner is like captaining your own vessel, and Stoicism becomes a powerful compass in these business waters.

Stoic Business Owners have a unique mindset. They don't just run a business; they run it with a touch of ancient philosophy. Picture it like a secret ingredient that adds wisdom, composure, and resilience to their entrepreneurial recipe.

Stoic Business Owners are decision-making wizards. They don't just flip a coin; they gather facts, consult experts, and ponder their choices. This wisdom ensures their decisions aren't just strong but also smart. In a world where speed often rules, they take their time, ensuring the path they choose is the right one.

Running a business isn't always smooth sailing. It's more like a rollercoaster ride with unexpected twists. Stoic Business Owners embrace these challenges. When the storm hits, they don't panic. Instead, they bounce back stronger, using setbacks for success.

What sets Stoic Business Owners apart isn't just their decision-making process; it's their ethical compass. They follow a code – a set of principles that guide them in doing what's right, not just for their pockets but for everyone involved. This commitment to fairness and integrity becomes the backbone of their business.

Being a business owner isn't just about making choices; it's about steering the team in the same direction. Stoic Business Owners excel in communication. They don't just announce changes; they explain the why, connecting decisions to the values that define their business. It's like being a captain who not only changes course but ensures the crew understands and believes in the new direction.

Stoic Business Owners grasp a fundamental truth – not everything is under their control. While they steer the ship, they acknowledge the unpredictable currents of the business world. Instead of resisting, they adapt. This acceptance of the uncontrollable gives them a unique edge, helping them navigate uncertainties with grace.

Stoic Business Owners lead by example. They don't just dictate; they roll up their sleeves and work alongside their team. This hands-on approach builds trust and creates a collaborative atmosphere where everyone feels valued.

The journey of a Stoic Business Owner is a continuous learning adventure. They believe in getting better every day. This mindset permeates their team, creating a culture where challenges are seen as opportunities to grow. By fostering this learning environment, Stoic Business Owners ensure their company stays agile and ready to face whatever challenges come their way.

These business owners aren't about flaunting success. They know they're not perfect and don't shy away from admitting mistakes. This humility not only makes them approachable but encourages their team to speak up and contribute ideas fearlessly.

Among more current leaders President Barack Obama is often seen to have demonstrated qualities of stoicism through his calm and collected demeanor, which some say echoes the political style of well-known stoic, Cato the Younger.

Stoicism transforms negative emotions into a sense of perspective and prepares you to have the right state of mind. At its heart it's about controlling things which are in your power to control and leaving the rest.

It requires being mindful, cultivating awareness and self-control, rather than being lost to emotion and random thought processes. Stoic exercises such as "practicing" misfortune and poverty help teach us that the worst-case situation is not in fact, the worst. And it can be great for business.

Stoic principles can build the resilience and state of mind required to rebound from knockbacks, so important in our new world of innovation and entrepreneurship.

Mary Kay Ash, the founder of Mary Kay Cosmetics, applied Stoic values in her business. She believed in making wise decisions, staying resilient in the face of challenges, and fostering a culture where everyone could succeed.

So, why should business owners embrace Stoicism? It's not just an ancient philosophy; it's a practical set of tools for building success.

1. **Making Informed Decisions:** Stoicism equips business owners to make decisions grounded in wisdom and foresight.
2. **Resilience in Challenges:** In the unpredictable business landscape, Stoicism provides the mental resilience needed to weather storms.
3. **Ethical Business Practices:** Following a Stoic code ensures fairness, integrity, and ethical conduct in business dealings.
4. **Effective Communication:** Stoic principles enhance communication, ensuring everyone in the company understands and aligns with the business's direction.

5. **Learning and Adaptability:** Embracing a Stoic mindset fosters a culture of continuous learning and adaptability, important for long-term success.

6. **Humble Leadership:** Stoicism encourages humility in leadership, creating an environment where collaboration and innovation thrive.

In the dynamic world of business, Stoic Business Owners stand out as captains who not only navigate the seas of entrepreneurship with wisdom and resilience but also inspire their crews to achieve greatness together.

Being a business owner is like sailing new waters. There's always a chance of hitting storms and facing rough seas. In the business world, risks are a constant companion. But here's a secret – some business owners, the Stoic ones, see risks not as obstacles but as opportunities for greater rewards.

Stoic Business Owners are not content with the status quo. They're pioneers, always seeking new horizons. Innovation often comes with risk, but it's a risk they willingly embrace. It's like setting sail to discover new lands – the journey might be uncertain, but the discoveries are worth it.

Imagine you're on a grand adventure, exploring unknown territories. As a business owner, you're like an explorer, charting new paths. Now, every path has its challenges, just like every business decision carries a level of risk. It's a bit like choosing between different routes – some might be smooth highways, and others bumpy trails.

Stoic Business Owners view risks through a unique lens. Instead of fearing them, they see risks as companions on their entrepreneurial journey. It's like knowing that the more challenging the path, the more breathtaking the view from the top.

Stoic Business Owners are not gamblers throwing dice to decide their fate. They are more like skilled chess players, thinking several moves ahead. Before taking risks, they calculate, analyze, and understand the game board (business landscape). It's not about taking blind chances; it's about making informed decisions.

Stoic Business Owners are not reckless daredevils. They believe in balance. It's about taking calculated risks, managing them wisely, and ensuring that the potential reward aligns with the mission and values of their business.

Sure, there's fear in taking risks. It's natural. But Stoic Business Owners don't let fear dictate their choices. Instead, they acknowledge the fear, understand it, and then move forward with courage. It's like standing on the edge of a cliff, knowing the jump is scary, but also knowing it leads to a magnificent waterfall.

Not every risk pays off. Sometimes, the path you choose might have unexpected twists. Stoic Business Owners understand this. When things don't go as planned, they don't crumble. Instead, they bounce back. Failure becomes not the end but a valuable lesson in their journey resulting in a new beginning.

Now, let's talk about rewards. Stoic Business Owners know that without risk, there's no triumph. It's like climbing a mountain – the summit is glorious because the climb was tough. The bigger the risk they take, the more satisfying the success becomes.

Throughout each situation, Stoic-minded business owners have left their mark. Think of them as pioneers who dared to venture where others hesitated.

Oprah Winfrey: From starting her own network to revolutionizing daytime television, Oprah took risks that reshaped the media industry.

In the world of Stoic Business Owners, risks aren't hurdles; they are thrilling adventures. Like a captain steering through stormy seas, these entrepreneurs navigate risks with wisdom, courage, and a long-term vision. It's not about avoiding the waves; it's about learning to ride them and, in the end, reaching new shores of success. So, fellow business adventurer, remember, the bigger the risk, the more magnificent the reward.

As a business owner embracing Stoicism, you're not just making decisions; you're wielding a powerful tool for fruitful and effective choices. Picture it as having the freedom to navigate your ship through new waters without the constant worry of the uncontrollable storms.

Stoicism grants you a unique kind of freedom – the freedom from being enslaved by worry. When faced with decisions, you don't carry the heavy burden of fearing what you can't control. It's like having a compass that points to wise choices, unaffected by the unpredictable winds.

In the world of Stoic decision-making, you are your own guide. There's no need to wait for someone else to tell you what's right or wrong. Your inner Stoic becomes a silent authority, offering counsel based on reason, virtue, and a deep understanding that some things are beyond your control.

While others might worry about the unknown, your Stoic mindset frees you. The fear of making mistakes doesn't paralyze you; it pushes you forward. You're not limited by the worry of the uncontrollable, allowing you to focus on what you can change and improve.

In the business arena, not everyone will understand your Stoic approach. Some might question your decisions. But here's the secret weapon – Stoicism acts as your shield. Criticism doesn't pierce through because you know your choices are grounded in reason and a commitment to virtuous principles.

Stoicism empowers you to be a self-reliant captain. You're not dependent on external validation or constant advice. While others may seek approval, you trust your ability to make decisions that align with your business's values and long-term goals.

Imagine a serene island of solitude in the middle of a stormy sea. That's your Stoic space. Here, you find strength in independence. The silence allows you to hear your inner wisdom, making decisions that aren't affected by external pressures.

Stoicism transforms your leadership style. You're not a commander shouting orders; you're a wise leader making decisions that resonate with authenticity. The freedom you experience flows through your team, creating an environment where everyone feels empowered to contribute their best.

The reward of your Stoic decisions isn't just financial success. It's the satisfaction of knowing you've steered your ship with wisdom and virtue. The fruits of your labor go beyond the balance sheet, extending to a sense of fulfillment and purpose.

In the unpredictable world of business, Stoicism becomes your innovative spirit. You're not afraid to venture into the unknown because you carry the Stoic mindset – embracing uncertainty as an inherent part of the business journey.

Being a business owner is like navigating new waters – full of risks and uncertainties. However, embracing Stoicism in your entrepreneurial journey can be your secret compass, guiding you with the freedom to make decisions that lead to fruitful rewards, all while shedding the weight of uncontrollable worries.

Stoicism is your business superpower. It doesn't just help you make decisions; it empowers you to make the right ones. Picture it as having a map that leads to success, free from the heavy clouds of concerns about things beyond your control.

As previously stated, in the Stoic world, you're not waiting for someone else to tell you what's right or wrong. Your inner Stoic becomes your guide, a silent advisor whispering wisdom based on reason and virtue. You're not seeking constant validation; you're trusting your judgment.

Others may be paralyzed by fear of the unknown, but not you. Stoicism releases you from the chains of worry. The fear of making mistakes doesn't weigh you down; it drives you forward. You focus on what you can change and improve, unburdened by the uncontrollable elements.

In the business field, criticism is inevitable. Stoicism acts as your shield. Criticisms bounce off because you know your decisions are grounded in reason and virtue. You're not swayed by external opinions; you're resolute in your commitment to your chosen path.

As you direct the business seas with Stoic freedom, remember this – your legacy isn't just in profits but in the example you set. Other business owners might wonder at your ability to make decisions without the weight of the uncontrollable, and, inspired, they too might set sail with the Stoic compass.

Stoicism provides a practical framework for business owners to navigate challenging situations and make sound decisions under pressure:

Situation 1:

A competitor launches a disruptive product, threatening market share.

Non-stoic business owner: Reacts with panic, engages in a price war, and may resort to unethical practices to regain market share.

Stoic business owner: Remains calm, analyzes the competitor's product, identifies its strengths and weaknesses, and develops a strategic response, potentially involving innovation or collaboration.

Situation 2:

An employee makes a costly mistake, leading to financial losses.

Non-stoic business owner: Blames the employee, reacts with anger, and may resort to punitive measures, damaging employee morale and productivity.

Stoic business owner: Understands that mistakes are inevitable, conducts a root cause analysis, identifies areas for improvement, provides constructive feedback to the employee, and implements measures to prevent similar occurrences.

Situation 3:

A customer raises ethical concerns about a supplier's practices.

Non-stoic business owner: May prioritize short-term gains, dismiss the concerns, and continue working with the supplier.

Stoic business owner: Takes the concerns seriously, investigates the supplier's practices, dialogues with the customer and the supplier, and takes appropriate action to uphold ethical standards and maintain stakeholder trust.

Situation 4:

A key employee expresses dissatisfaction with their position and threatens to leave the company.

Non-stoic business owner: Reacts with defensiveness, may attempt to coerce the employee to stay, and fails to address the underlying reasons for their dissatisfaction.

Stoic business owner: Listens attentively to the employee's concerns, acknowledges their contributions, engages in open and honest communication, and explores potential solutions, such as role adjustments or career development opportunities, to address their dissatisfaction and retain their talent.

Situation 5:

A customer experiences a product malfunction that leads to negative online reviews and a tarnished brand reputation.

Non-stoic business owner: Reacts with anger and frustration, blames the customer, engages in a defensive public response, and fails to take immediate action to address the issue.

Stoic business owner: Maintains composure, apologizes sincerely to the customer, initiates a thorough investigation to identify the root cause of the malfunction, promptly issues a product recall or repair plan, and communicates transparently with the public to restore trust and mitigate reputational damage.

Situation 6:

A conflict arises between two departments, hindering collaboration and productivity.

Non-stoic business owner: Ignores the conflict, allowing it to escalate and affect overall operations, or attempts to impose a solution without addressing the underlying causes of the disagreement.

Stoic business owner: Acknowledges the conflict and its potential impact, facilitates open communication between the departments, mediates the situation with impartiality, and encourages a collaborative approach to resolve the underlying issues and restore harmony.

Situation 7:

An industry-wide economic downturn significantly impacts the company's revenue and profitability.

Non-stoic business owner: Panics, makes impulsive decisions to cut costs, and may resort to unethical practices to maintain profits.

Stoic business owner: Remains calm, analyzes the market trends and the company's financial position, develops a strategic response plan involving cost-efficiency measures, product diversification, or expansion into new markets, and communicates transparently with employees and stakeholders to maintain confidence and morale.

Situation 8:

A new technological advancement disrupts the industry, posing a threat to the company's competitive edge.

Non-stoic business owner: Denies the potential impact of the technology, resists change, and fails to adapt the company's strategy.

Stoic business owner: Embraces the disruptive technology, analyzes its potential applications, invests in research and development, and adapts the company's products, services, and business processes to stay ahead of the curve and maintain its competitive position.

To conclude, small business owners can benefit from absorbing the principles of stoicism into their management style. By accepting constants, focusing on your span of control, practicing mindfulness, and embracing constant (often chaotic) and inevitable change, business owners can improve their management skills and lead their businesses to success.

"Everything we hear is an opinion, not a fact."

Marcus Aurelius

So, fellow businessmen, adopt the freedom that Stoicism brings to your decision-making. Sail confidently, knowing that your Stoic wisdom will guide you to rewarding shores, regardless of the storms you might encounter along the way.

Chapter 9

Stoic Community Leaders

*E*ver since the evolution of mankind, humans have always deviated towards living in a community and with one of their kind. A strong and supportive community can provide any individual a sense of belonging, purpose, and security in this lonesome world. In a world where social isolation and loneliness are becoming increasingly established, it's essential to explore different approaches to community building. One such approach is the use of Stoic philosophy.

Leadership requires a range of qualities that adopt effective decision-making, empathy, resilience, and moral guidance. An ancient philosophical school of thought that offers valuable insights and practices for leaders is Stoicism. Rooted in classical

Greece and Rome, Stoicism teaches self-control, acceptance of fate, and the prioritization of virtues over external factors. By adopting Stoic principles, leaders cultivate a strong and adaptive mindset, enabling the navigation of complex situations and leading their teams to success.

Now, let's learn about being a community leader with a touch of Stoicism. You know, being that person who guides, supports, and makes things better for everyone.

The year 2020 etched itself into our collective memory as a stark reminder of the ever-present uncertainty facing the global community. The pandemic served as a catalyst, exposing the fragility of our lives and economies while simultaneously highlighting the crucial role of leadership in navigating such unprecedented challenges.

To steer individuals and organizations into new ground in today's quickly evolving world, marked by constant flux and upheaval, leaders must exhibit a unique blend of agility and purpose. The demands of a changing global political landscape, social trends, economic shocks, technological breakthroughs, and the nature of labor itself necessitate a reinvention of leadership that places an emphasis on adaptability, resilience, and a sincere dedication to the greater good

There will be a growing need for morally sound, capable, and impartial leaders as the world's population grows, the climate shifts, and the demand for natural resources rises. The ageless wisdom of stoic philosophy offers a crucial prism through which to understand and rethink leadership for the twenty-first century in this chaotic world.

The foundational idea of stoicism is interconnectivity. We are all members of the same human race, as the Stoics remind us. Based on these fundamental yet profound observations, they asserted that every person plays a significant role. Nature, in its inherent wisdom, encourages cooperation within each species to ensure its continuation.

While ants and bees instinctively work together towards a collective goal, humans, with their complex minds influenced by individual societal conditioning, require a conscious effort to discern reality from the lens of their unique experiences. By employing reason as our guide, we can pierce through the veil of personal biases and recognize our inherent connection to humanity. This recognition forms the foundation of Stoic leadership, urging us to act in accordance with the principles of the common good.

The Stoics employed a powerful metaphor to illustrate the interconnectedness of humanity. They envisioned humanity as a single body, with each individual acting as a limb, contributing to the overall health and well-being. This metaphor emphasizes the shared responsibility we hold for the collective good. Just as each limb contributes to the smooth functioning of the body, so too must we contribute our unique talents and abilities to the greater good of our species.

That being said, this high standard is not meant to be scary or demoralizing. Rather, it serves as a catalyst for action, encouraging us to harmonize our actions with the natural order. The Stoics believed that working for the common good eventually helps each of us personally. By linking ourselves with the natural order of things and improving the well-being of others, we can develop a sense of purpose and contentment.

The Stoics firmly believed that human fulfillment is inextricably linked to contributing to the common good. By acting virtuously, we cultivate internal harmony and experience the distinctive hallmarks of living in accordance with nature – freedom from negative emotions, a sense of flow, and genuine happiness. These internal qualities then manifest in our outward actions, benefiting those around us and contributing to the positive trajectory of society as a whole.

The pursuit of virtue encompasses a range of qualities essential for effective leadership. These include courage, wisdom, justice, temperance, and a commitment to reason and fairness. By cultivating these virtues, leaders can inspire trust and confidence, fostering a collaborative and productive environment. They can make ethical and well-informed decisions, prioritizing the long-term well-being of the organization and its stakeholders. They can also navigate conflict with grace and composure, working towards solutions that benefit all parties involved.

In the face of uncertainty and change, the Stoic principles offer invaluable guidance for leaders. By embracing interconnectedness and prioritizing the common good, leaders can develop the resilience and agility necessary to navigate constant flux. By cultivating virtue and acting ethically, they can inspire others and build trust, fostering a sense of shared purpose within their organizations.

The principles of Stoic leadership hold particular relevance in today's dynamic world. Leaders who embrace these principles can navigate the complexities of the 21st century with wisdom, courage, and compassion, building a brighter future for all.

As we navigate the complexities of the 21st century, the principles of Stoicism offer valuable insights for leadership development. By embracing the interconnectedness of humanity and prioritizing the common good, leaders can cultivate resilience, agility, and purpose – qualities essential for navigating a constantly changing world. With Stoicism as a guiding light, leaders can inspire others, build trust, and create a world where individuals and organizations thrive, together.

Stoic community leaders bring a number of good things to the table:

1. **Cool Under Pressure:**

They stay calm when things get crazy, which helps everyone feel more relaxed.

2. **Sorting Out Conflicts:**

Instead of ignoring problems, they face them, turning issues into chances for the community to grow.

3. **Dealing with Criticism:**

When the community faces criticism, they handle it smartly, protecting our reputation and making us stronger.

4. **Connecting with Young People:**

They're open to new ideas and talk with the younger generation, making our community livelier and broader.

5. Emergency Ready:

Stoics don't panic in tough times. They already have everything planned out in case of an emergency which makes them ready for everything.

6. Celebrating Differences:

They appreciate everyone's uniqueness, making sure our community is a friendly place for everyone.

7. Keeping Volunteers Happy:

When volunteers feel overwhelmed, they talk about it openly and find solutions together, so everyone stays happy and motivated.

8. Dreaming Big for Us:

These leaders don't just discuss the future as a mere plan ahead; they paint the whole picture of how wonderful a community built on their ideals would be so it makes the people excited to be a part of their world. Hence, it's important for them to be great communicators so they can lay out their whole plan in front of the world effectively.

Stoicism is not one of those philosophies that have gotten outdated with time. Stoic philosophy is a practical philosophy which can be implemented in community activities even today.

Here are some ways that Stoic practices can be used to support the development of a community:

The essence of stoicism is getting to know oneself—inside and out. It's similar to having a long talk with yourself to discover what motivates you. However, going it alone can be difficult; that's where the community can help.

Imagine spending time with your friends and having genuine conversations about your feelings and thoughts rather than just chatting about the newest TikTok trends. That is the main goal of stoic organizations. It's a safe place to be vulnerable, talk about your worries and challenges, and encourage one another along this life's journey.

But these meetings involve more than just conversation—there's this thing called meditation. It's like going on a mental vacation where you concentrate on your breathing and block out all other sounds. It's like a mental health physical examination! This increases your awareness of your thoughts, feelings, and even your physical state!

You begin to gain a deeper understanding of yourself by being aware of what's happening inside of you. You understand why you respond to things in a particular way and how your emotions and ideas can affect the people in your life. It's similar to deciphering a secret code that only you know.

Stoicism involves more than just introspection; it also entails serving those in your immediate vicinity. Consider it as giving back good karma. And there's no better way to accomplish that than by giving back to your community and volunteering?

The possibilities are endless, ranging from planning a fundraiser for that animal shelter you adore to tidying up the park where you frequently hang out. Plus, it's like creating your own Stoic army when you collaborate with others on these projects. You get to spend time together, meet new people, and feel good about improving your town.

Not only is it beneficial to others, but it is also beneficial to you. Living in harmony with the natural world and our community is a core principle of stoicism. By doing your part to make your surroundings cleaner and greener, you're basically honoring that principle.

Education is an essential component of Stoicism. By organizing educational workshops and seminars on Stoic philosophy, communities can promote personal growth and self-awareness among its members.

These workshops can cover a range of topics, from the hiSituation of Stoicism to practical applications of Stoic principles in everyday life. They can also include interactive activities and exercises that help community members develop their understanding of Stoicism.

Stoicism places a strong emphasis on reason and rationality. Communities can use this principle to promote healthy conflict resolution strategies and mediation techniques that provide a safe space for disagreements to be resolved.

Community members can learn techniques for active listening, effective communication, and collaborative problem-solving. By practicing these techniques, they can develop a deeper understanding of each other's perspectives and work together to find mutually beneficial solutions.

Just like in business, Stoicism brings a lot of practical benefits to community leaders:

Learned Decisions: Stoicism helps community leaders make effective decisions.

Strength in Challenges: It provides mental resilience during tough times.

Ethical Conduct: Following Stoic principles ensures fairness and integrity.

Effective Communication: Stoicism enhances communication for better understanding.

Learning and Adaptability: A Stoic mindset fosters a culture of continuous learning.

Humble Leadership: Stoicism encourages leaders to be humble, making collaboration and innovation thrive.

Imagine being the leader everyone looks up to because you lead with wisdom, strength, and a deep sense of fairness. That's the power of being a Stoic Community Leader.

Imagine being the person in your community who doesn't just decide on an urge but takes the time to think things through. Stoic Community Leaders are like decision-making wizards. They gather information, talk to experts, and really consider their choices. It's not about being quick; it's about being smart and making decisions that truly help the community.

Being a community leader isn't always easy. Sometimes, it's like riding a rollercoaster with unexpected turns. Stoic leaders don't freak out when challenges show up. They tackle them head-on and come out even stronger. Instead of seeing problems as barriers, they view them as opportunities to succeed.

What sets Stoic Community Leaders apart is not just how they make decisions but why they make them. They follow a set of principles – a code of ethics. It's like having a rule book that says, "Do what's right, not just for you but for everyone." This ethical approach becomes the backbone of their leadership.

As a community leader, it's not just about giving orders; it's about making sure everyone is on the same page. Stoic Community Leaders excel in communication. They don't just announce changes; they explain why those changes matter. It's like being a captain who doesn't just steer the ship but makes sure the team understands and believes in the journey.

Stoic Community Leaders get a fundamental truth – not everything is under their control. While they guide the ship, they know there are unpredictable waves. Instead of fighting against them, they adapt. This ability to accept the unpredictable gives them a unique edge in handling whatever comes their way.

Stoic Community Leaders don't just talk the talk; they walk the walk. They don't sit back and give orders; they roll up their sleeves and work alongside the community. This hands-on approach builds trust and creates an atmosphere where everyone feels valued and involved.

Leading a community is like being on a continuous learning journey. Stoic Community Leaders believe in getting better every day. This mindset spreads through the community, creating an environment where challenges are seen as opportunities to grow. By encouraging this learning spirit, Stoic Leaders make sure their community stays strong and ready for whatever comes their way.

These leaders aren't about showing off success. They know they're not perfect and aren't afraid to admit mistakes. This humbleness makes them approachable and encourages everyone in the community to speak up and contribute ideas without fear.

Leaders who embrace stoicism don't take things personally. They own what's in their control and don't waste energy worrying about what others think, say, or do. Freed up energy means more mental space to stay focused on your goals. Plus, not taking things personally can go a long way when it comes to navigating workplace conflict productively.

Stoics practiced the art of acquiescence, the idea of accepting things you can't control as is – including problems and challenges. The productivity benefit, Instead of pushing against the struggle and feeling even more stuck, you'll see things more clearly and thus become more open to constructive solutions and creative next moves.

It's normal to experience emotions. Stoicism is not about being emotionless, but about being aware of your emotional state and how it's affecting you (and your productivity). Stoic leaders are more energized by a meeting gone wrong or a difficult conversation because they observe their emotions about the event instead of letting them get the best of their entire day or week.

This attitude also helps them approach failure in a productive way – stoic leaders expect failure and see it as a stepping stone to learning and opportunities.

Stoics believe in a growth mindset: failure as a foundation to growth. Startups embrace the idea of failure as an integral part of the path to discovery. Failing fast is productive because it saves costs and other resources in the long run.

This means that they are able to assess their goals and progress productively too. Stoic leaders don't get discouraged when they fail to meet a quarterly team objective. They accept what is and focus on assessing the situation objectively, which allows them to keep going and adjust their plan accordingly.

The Stoics believed in the pursuit of a virtuous life. This pursuit, by definition, takes place through consistent efforts over the course of a lifetime. Stoic leaders play the long game too when it comes to their work goals—stepping away from the ditches of your daily work for at least a few moments every day to connect to the bigger picture of why you do what you do, and where you are ultimately going. You'll be more focused on what matters the most as a result, and your productivity will skyrocket.

Being a community leader is like being a guide for a group of people, helping them move forward and make things better. Imagine if the person in charge was always negative and let outside things control their decisions. That wouldn't be so helpful, right? That's why community leaders should use something called stoicism.

Think of stoicism as a tool for community leaders. It helps them not get stuck in a loop of negativity. When leaders constantly think about bad stuff and let it control their decisions, it's not good for the community. Stoicism is like a shield against that negativity.

The main job of a community leader is to guide their community towards a brighter future. If a leader is always bogged down by negativity and lets outside things cloud their judgment, they won't be very helpful. That's why it's important for community leaders to bring stoicism into their lives. Let's see how this plays out in eight everyday situations.

Situation 1:

The Budget Blues

A non-stoic leader might panic when the community faces financial challenges.

A stoic leader, however, stays calm, judges the situation, and communicates openly about the necessary changes. They focus on solutions, inspiring confidence in the community.

Situation 2:

Neighborhood Conflicts

When conflicts arise among community members, a non-stoic leader might avoid addressing the issue.

A stoic leader tackles it head-on, facilitating open communication. They turn conflicts into opportunities for understanding and growth, fostering a harmonious community.

Situation 3:

External Criticism

If the community faces criticism from outside, a non-stoic leader may react defensively.

A stoic leader acknowledges the criticism, evaluates it objectively, and communicates a well-thought-out response. This approach preserves the community's reputation and builds resilience.

Situation 4:

Youth Engagement

In engaging with the youth, a non-stoic leader might struggle to relate or dismiss new ideas.

A stoic leader, on the other hand, embraces change, listens to the younger generation, and communicates a shared vision, creating an inclusive and dynamic community.

Situation 5:

Emergency Preparedness

Facing a crisis, a non-stoic leader might succumb to panic.

A stoic leader remains composed, communicates a clear plan, and involves the community in preparation. This builds trust and makes sure everyone is ready to face challenges together.

Situation 6:

Celebrating Diversity

A non-stoic leader might ignore or undermine the importance of diversity.

A stoic leader, however, values differences, communicates the significance of diversity, and fosters an inclusive environment. This promotes unity and understanding in the community.

Situation 7:

Volunteer Burnout

When volunteers feel overwhelmed, a non-stoic leader may not address the issue, risking burnout.

A stoic leader communicates openly, acknowledges the challenges, and collaboratively finds solutions. This approach maintains a motivated and dedicated volunteer base.

Situation 8:

Vision for the Future

A non-stoic leader might struggle to convey a clear vision for the community's future.

A stoic leader communicates a compelling vision, aligns it with shared values, and engages the community in the journey. This promotes a sense of purpose and optimism.

In all these situations, the common thread is communication. Stoic community leaders prioritize clear, open, and honest communication. It's not just about talking; it's about connecting, listening, facing challenges together, and aligning actions with values. Communication becomes the foundation for building a resilient, positive, and united community.

Stoicism is a way of thinking that can help us deal with tough situations, challenges, or failures. It teaches us to accept things as they are and to focus on how we react to them instead of getting stuck on what happened.

In times of personal struggles or problems, Stoicism can help you stay calm and strong during difficult times. It can provide a structure for how to keep your emotions in check and be more resilient. At the same time, leadership skills may not directly apply.

Suppose one is dealing with high stress or anxiety, primarily due to factors outside their control. In that case, the principles of Stoicism can be particularly beneficial.

Leadership skills are important in situations that require guiding a team or organization towards a common goal.

Effective communication and conflict resolution are crucial leadership skills when dealing with conflicts in a team or group setting.

If you're in a position where proactive change is required, whether in a business, a community, or a project, leadership is more effective than stoicism.

Leadership qualities are essential when it's necessary to inspire and motivate others. Stoicism is a philosophy that mainly concentrates on self-improvement. While it can encourage others by being a good example, it may not have a direct impact on them. However, when pursuing clear and visible objectives, especially in a professional setting, leadership skills such as strategic planning, delegation, and decision-making are essential.

When it comes to advancing your career and growing professionally, being a good leader is often more important than just following strict rules and principles.

The Stoic philosophy holds within its core a profound understanding of global citizenship, encompassing the entirety of humankind. Ancient Stoics identified themselves as "citizens of the world," transcending the artificial constructs of political, economic, and social boundaries. These barriers, in their view, were ultimately irrational impediments to human cooperation, hindering our collective potential. As Marcus Aurelius eloquently stated, "We were born into this world to work together like the feet, hands, eyelids, or upper and lower rows of teeth" (Meditations 2.1). This potent metaphor of the human body underscores the fundamental interconnectedness of all individuals, serving as a constant reminder that our individual well-being is inextricably linked to the well-being of the whole.

This emphasis on community lies at the very heart of Stoic philosophy. The mental practices meticulously developed by the Stoics aimed to empower individuals to not only endure any circumstance but to thrive in the face of adversity. By cultivating inner freedom from the constraints of external circumstances, we equip ourselves to act with virtue and contribute positively to the world around us. While individual impact may often appear limited, the collective effort of individuals, each doing their "one tiny thing," has the potential to create significant and lasting positive change. Even if the desired outcome is not immediately achieved, the very act of practicing Stoicism and striving for the common good represents a significant victory in itself.

Today's world is marked by an unprecedented degree of interconnectedness on a global scale, so the Stoic emphasis on community has great resonance. Adopting the principles of Stoic cosmopolitanism can help us promote a sense of group action and shared responsibility. Thus, a society that is more compassionate, resilient, and inclusive is made possible.

The stoic perspective pushes us to think about the bigger picture of our actions rather than just our own accomplishments.

We can rise above self-interest and help create a better future for everyone by realizing our interconnectedness and putting the common good first. This rethought concept of community, which is based on the timeless ideas of stoicism, provides a potent remedy for the isolation and fragmentation that are frequently features of contemporary life. By acknowledging our common humanity and working together, we can create a world where individuals and communities not only survive but thrive, collectively and individually.

Chapter 10

NPO Leadership and Stoicism

S toicism emphasizes virtue, reason, and resilience and offers valuable insights for Non-Profit Organization leaders. Non-profit leaders face unique challenges as they cross the complexities of social issues and the emotional demands of their work. Stoicism, with its importance on mental strength and resilience, provides valuable tools for NPO leaders to face these challenges with composure and maintain their commitment to their cause.

Imagine a warrior, clothed in solid armor, facing a difficult battle. This armor protects them from physical harm, allowing them to fight effectively and defend their values. In the same way, Stoicism equips NPO leaders with mental strength, acting as an armor against the emotional and psychological challenges they encounter.

Core Stoic Principles for NPO Leadership

Stoicism provides a framework for NPO leaders to cultivate the qualities and behaviors necessary for effective leadership. Here are some key Stoic principles that can be applied to NPO leadership:

Honesty: Stoics believe that the highest goal in life is to live in accordance with honesty. For NPO leaders, this means embodying values such as compassion, integrity, and justice in their decision-making and actions.

Reason: Stoics emphasize the importance of using reason to guide one's thoughts and actions. NPO leaders can apply reason to make sound decisions, analyze complex situations, and develop effective strategies.

Resilience: Stoics teach that we cannot control external events, but we can control our own reactions to them. NPO leaders can cultivate resilience by developing emotional intelligence, managing stress, and maintaining a positive outlook when beset by unanticipated external challenges.

Benefits of Stoicism for NPO Leadership

Adopting Stoic principles can bring several benefits to NPO leadership:

- Enhanced Decision-Making: Stoic principles can help NPO leaders make more informed and ethical decisions, considering all stakeholders and potential consequences.

- Effective Communication: Stoicism promotes clear, concise, and respectful communication, which is essential for building strong relationships with staff, volunteers, donors, and beneficiaries.

- Empowering Leadership: Stoic principles encourage empowering others and fostering a culture of collaboration and shared responsibility within the NPO.

- Managing Challenges: Stoicism provides a framework for coping with setbacks, maintaining composure under pressure, and adapting to changing circumstances.

- Focus on the Present Moment: Instead of dwelling on past failures or worrying about the future, focus on making the most of the present and taking positive action.

- Virtue-Based Decision Making: Basing decisions on principles like justice, compassion, equity and wisdom ensures alignment with your values and the organization's mission.

Practical Application of Stoicism in NPO Leadership

NPO leaders can incorporate Stoic principles into their daily leadership practices in several ways:

- Self-Reflection: Regularly engage in self-reflection to assess one's own thoughts, emotions, and behaviors, and identify areas for improvement.
- Perspective-Taking: Seek to understand the perspectives of others, including staff, volunteers, beneficiaries, and stakeholders.
- Emotional Regulation: Practice techniques such as mindfulness and meditation to manage stress and cultivate emotional resilience.
- Focus on Controllables: Focus on what is within one's control, such as one's own actions, attitudes, and decision-making.
- Accept Uncertainty: Embrace uncertainty as a natural part of life and avoid dwelling on things that cannot be controlled.

Emotional Challenges in NPO Leadership with Stoicism

Non-profit organizations tackle complex and sensitive issues, often working with vulnerable populations facing various challenges. This emotionally demanding work can leave NPO leaders vulnerable to distress, anxiety, and even depression. Recognizing and addressing these emotional challenges is essential for their well-being and the effectiveness of their leadership.

- Stoicism, an ancient philosophy, offers valuable tools for navigating emotional challenges in NPO leadership. By focusing on quality, reason, and resilience, Stoicism trains leaders with the mental framework and practical strategies to manage stress, maintain emotional well-being, and lead with wisdom and compassion.

- Dichotomy of Control: Recognizing the characteristic between things within our control (thoughts, actions, reactions) and things beyond our control (external events, others' behavior). This helps change focus from worrying about uncontrollable factors to directing energy towards what can be influenced.

- Acceptance and Surrender: Accepting what is outside our control allows us to let go of unnecessary anxieties and frustrations. This does not imply resignation, but rather a calm acceptance of reality as it is, creating space for proactive and effective response.

- Perspective-Taking: Cultivating the ability to see things from different perspectives, including those of beneficiaries, colleagues, and stakeholders. This promotes empathy, understanding, and reduces judgment, leading to more constructive communication and problem-solving.
- Mindfulness and Meditation: Practicing mindfulness through meditation and other techniques can help NPO leaders become more aware of their thoughts and emotions, allowing them to observe and analyze them without judgment, thereby reducing the impact of negative emotions.
- Focus on the Present Moment: Stoicism emphasizes focusing on the present moment, rather than dwelling on the past or worrying about the future. This promotes a sense of calm and clarity, enabling leaders to make decisions and take action based on current realities, rather than anxieties or regrets.

A Stoic leader in the non-profit sector sets an example for the team. They lead with virtue, integrity, and a deep sense of purpose. This principle creates a positive organizational culture that can weather emotional challenges.

- Reduced Stress and Anxiety: Stoic principles and practices help NPO leaders manage stress and anxiety, lowering the risk of burnout and promoting emotional well-being.

- Improved Decision-Making: Emotional clarity and a lack of judgment lead to more reasoned and informed decision-making, benefiting both the NPO and its receivers.

- Enhanced Leadership Effectiveness: Stoic leaders inspire trust and confidence through their calm and composed demeanor, adopting strong relationships and improving collaboration within the organization.

- Greater Compassion and Empathy: Stoicism encourages seeing things from others' perspectives, leading to greater compassion and empathy for beneficiaries and colleagues, enhancing the quality of service and support provided.

- Wise Decision-Making: By focusing on reason and logic, Stoicism helps NPO leaders make well-informed decisions, even under pressure. They are able to objectively analyze situations, consider different perspectives, and avoid impulsiveness, leading to better outcomes for the organization and the people they serve.

- Compassionate Leadership: Stoicism emphasizes understanding and empathy towards others. NPO leaders develop a deeper understanding of the challenges faced by their beneficiaries and colleagues, enabling them to provide more effective support and leadership with greater compassion and care.

- Maintaining Motivation: Working in the social sector can be emotionally draining at times. Stoicism teaches NPO leaders to find meaning and purpose in their work, even amidst challenges. By focusing on the greater good and the positive impact they are making, they can sustain their motivation and commitment to the cause.

Just as a warrior must train and practice to become skilled in battle, NPO leaders can strengthen their Stoic armor through various practices:

- Self-Reflection: Regularly reflecting on thoughts, feelings, and actions helps identify areas for improvement and develop greater self-awareness.
- Mindfulness and Meditation: These practices train the mind to focus on the present moment, reducing stress and enhancing emotional control.
- Journaling: Writing down thoughts and experiences can help process emotions, gain perspective, and make sense of challenging situations.

- Studying Stoic Texts: Reading and reflecting on the wisdom of Stoic philosophers like Marcus Aurelius and Epictetus provides valuable insights and practical guidance.

Non-profit organizations operate in complex environments, often confronting societal issues that evoke strong emotions. NPO leaders face a unique set of challenges, ranging from resource constraints and operational difficulties to dealing with the struggles and suffering of those they serve. These challenges can take a toll on their emotional well-being and threaten to erode their commitment to their cause.

Imagine yourself as the leader of an NPO dedicated to providing meals for homeless youth. Every day, you face heartbreaking stories of hardship and struggle. Witnessing the pain and suffering of those you serve can take a toll on your emotions, leading to feelings of frustration, sadness, and even despair.

During these emotional challenges, it's important to maintain composure and commitment to your cause. This is where Stoicism can be a powerful tool. By applying its principles, NPO leaders can navigate difficult situations with wisdom and resilience, ensuring their own well-being and the effectiveness of their organization.

NPOs often face public inquiry and criticism, particularly when dealing with sensitive issues. This can lead to feelings of doubt, defensiveness, and even anger. Stoicism can help NPO leaders respond to criticism constructively by focusing on the validity of the critique, accepting responsibility for mistakes, and demonstrating openness to improvement. This allows them to learn from criticism, strengthen their organization, and maintain public trust.

NPOs often operate with limited resources, requiring leaders to make tough decisions about resource distribution. This can lead to stress and anxiety as leaders strive to fulfill their mission with limited funding. Stoicism encourages prioritizing needs over wants, focusing on efficient resource utilization, and being creative in finding solutions with limited funds. This allows NPO leaders to maximize their impact and remain fiscally responsible.

The dedication and passion required for NPO leadership can sometimes blur the lines between work and personal life. This can lead to burnout and strain on personal relationships. Stoicism emphasizes the importance of self-care and setting boundaries. By prioritizing time for rest and rejuvenation, NPO leaders can maintain their own well-being, prevent burnout, and show up with renewed energy and focus for both their work and personal life.

NPO leaders need to inspire and motivate their team members, volunteers, and stakeholders to work towards their mission. This can be challenging, especially when faced with setbacks or discouraging situations. Stoicism encourages focusing on shared values and goals, recognizing and celebrating achievements, and fostering a sense of community and belonging. This helps create a positive and motivated environment where everyone feels valued and contributes towards a greater purpose.

NPOs might not always get the results they want, even with their best efforts. Feelings of disappointment, annoyance, and even failure may result from this. NPO leaders who practice stoicism find it easier to accept that they cannot control everything and are motivated to concentrate on their efforts and advancements rather than obsessing over things that are unchangeable. Even when results are not perfect, NPO leaders can still have a positive impact by learning from mistakes and changing their strategy.

These circumstances also show how NPO leaders can use stoicism as a useful tool to help them navigate the emotional complexities of their work and foster effective leadership that benefits the communities they serve as well as the organization.

Scenario 1:

Facing Funding Challenges

Non-Stoic Leader: Panics, blames external factors, cuts 'non-essential' services.

Stoic Leader: Remains calm, assesses the situation, prioritizes, communicates transparently. Focuses on resourceful solutions and fundraising strategies.

Scenario 2:

Managing Staff Conflicts

Non-Stoic Leader: Avoids the issue, fosters resentment, productivity declines. Possibly creates a 'we-they' environment.

Stoic Leader: Facilitates open communication, encourages active listening and understanding. Focuses on resolving issues constructively and fostering a positive work environment.

Scenario 3:

Experiencing Criticism and Public Inquiry

Non-Stoic Leader: Reacts defensively, damages reputation, loses trust.

Stoic Leader: Acknowledges criticism objectively, evaluates its validity, responds thoughtfully. Focuses on learning from mistakes and improving operations.

Scenario 4:

Engaging with Diverse Communities

Non-Stoic Leader: Ignores or dismisses differences, delays community growth.

Stoic Leader: Values diversity, encourages open dialogue, builds inclusive programs. Focuses on adopting a sense of belonging and promoting mutual understanding.

Scenario 5:

Motivating Volunteers and Staff

Non-Stoic Leader: Relies on extrinsic rewards, burnout occurs, enthusiasm diminishes.

Stoic Leader: Inspires through shared purpose and values, recognizes contributions. Focuses on creating a meaningful work environment and fostering a sense of accomplishment.

Scenario 6:

Setting and Achieving Goals

Non-Stoic Leader: Sets unrealistic goals, becomes discouraged by setbacks, gives up easily.

Stoic Leader: Sets SMART goals, remains focused on progress, learns from failures. Focuses on continuous improvement and celebrating small wins along the way.

Scenario 7:

Facing Personal Challenges and Loss

Non-Stoic Leader: Neglects self-care, loses focus, reduces effectiveness.

Stoic Leader: Prioritizes self-care and well-being, seeks support, and maintains resilience. Focuses on managing emotions and returning to leadership with renewed strength.

Scenario 8:

Celebrating Successes and Achievements

Non-Stoic Leader: Takes full credit, encourages competition, creates an unhealthy work environment.

Stoic Leader: Shares credit with team, celebrates collaboratively, promotes a culture of appreciation. Focuses on recognizing individual contributions and maintaining a sense of shared purpose.

Leading a nonprofit organization (NPO) is a special kind of job. It's not just about making money; it's about making a positive impact on the world. And to do this well, NPO leaders can learn a lot from Stoicism.

1. Helping Others

NPOs exist to help people or causes. Stoicism teaches that helping others is a noble and fulfilling purpose. NPO leaders, by focusing on the well-being of others, align with Stoic principles.

2. Staying Calm in Challenges

Running an NPO comes with challenges—funding issues, unexpected events, and more. Stoicism encourages leaders to stay calm in tough situations. Instead of panicking, a Stoic NPO leader thinks clearly to find solutions.

3. Facing Criticism with Grace

NPOs might face criticism, whether it's about their impact or how they operate. Stoicism guides leaders to face criticism with grace. They evaluate it objectively, learn from it, and use it to improve.

4. Communication is Key

Clear communication is vital for NPOs. Stoicism emphasizes effective communication, ensuring that everyone involved understands the mission and values. This helps in building trust and support.

5. Adapting to Change

The world changes, and so do the needs of the people an NPO serves. Stoicism teaches leaders to accept change and adapt. NPO leaders, with a Stoic mindset, can navigate changes effectively.

6. Unity in Diversity

NPOs often deal with diverse communities. Stoicism encourages the appreciation of differences. A Stoic NPO leader fosters an inclusive environment, recognizing the unique strengths each person brings.

7. Motivating Volunteers

Volunteers are the backbone of many NPOs. Stoicism helps leaders understand and motivate volunteers effectively. By acknowledging challenges openly and finding solutions together, a Stoic leader keeps the team motivated.

8. Building a Vision for the Future

NPOs work for a better future. Stoic leaders don't just plan; they paint a picture of what the future could be. A clear vision inspires everyone involved, making them feel part of something important.

There's a misconception that paints Marcus Aurelius, the Roman emperor and Stoic philosopher, as a misanthrope. This perception stems from his apparent focus on negativity in "Meditations," where he contemplates betrayal, meddling, and deceit. However, attributing this negativity to misanthropy would be a misinterpretation of his philosophical perspective.

Instead of harboring ill will towards others, Marcus engages in a deliberate mental exercise. He cultivates a particular type of empathy, a "philosophical attitude toward humanity," that embraces our inherent flaws and imperfections. He acknowledges that everyone, including himself, possesses the potential for both wisdom and vice.

This perspective is rooted in the Stoic concept of "natural affection," a love akin to that between parents and children or siblings. It echoes the paternal love of Zeus, whom the Stoics viewed as the father of all mankind. They sought to anticipate the shortcomings of others without judgment, blame, or anger. This preemptive understanding allowed them to respond with compassion and grace when faced with others' imperfections.

Marcus doesn't explicitly state this, but his writings are infused with this paradoxical view of humanity. He recognizes that, despite our flaws and vulnerabilities, we all hold the potential for good. This fundamental belief underpins his commitment to social virtue, justice, fairness, and kindness. His "Meditations" are not a testament to misanthropy, but rather a philosophical journey towards developing a healthy and harmonious attitude towards all human beings, warts and all.

By reframing our understanding of Marcus' perspective, we gain a deeper appreciation for his philosophy and its relevance to our lives. His teachings encourage us to move beyond superficial judgments and recognize the shared humanity that connects us all. In doing so, we can cultivate empathy, compassion, and a deeper understanding of ourselves and others, ultimately contributing to a more just and harmonious society.

Stoicism for NPO leaders is not just about coping with challenges, but about finding meaning and purpose in their work. By embracing Stoic principles, NPO leaders can improve the qualities and behaviors necessary to navigate the challenges and opportunities of leading a nonprofit organization. Stoicism can empower NPO leaders to make a positive impact on the world while maintaining their own well-being and resilience.

Embracing Stoicism is a continuous journey of self-reflection, practice, and learning. NPO leaders can include these principles into their daily lives through various practices like journaling, meditation, and incorporating Stoic quotes and wisdom into their conversations and decision-making processes. By adding Stoicism into their leadership approach, NPO leaders can help emotional resilience, navigate challenges with wisdom, and ultimately contribute more effectively to the cause they champion. Remember, Stoicism is not about becoming emotionless, but rather about managing emotions constructively and living a life of purpose and meaning in the face of adversity. By consistently applying Stoicism, NPO leaders can build the mental strength needed to navigate the demanding world of non-profit work, fulfill their mission with unwavering commitment, and leave a lasting positive impact on the world.

Stoicism, of course, may not appeal to or work for everyone. It is a rather demanding philosophy of life, where your moral character is ordered to be the only truly worthy thing to develop in life i.e., health, education, and even wealth.

Chapter 11

Stoic Political Leadership

*T*he idea of transcending feelings and desires in politics is a complex and multifaceted one, with arguments for both for and against its feasibility and desirability. Here are some key considerations.

Arguments for transcending feelings

and desires in politics

Eliminating emotions and personal preferences from policy decisions is intriguing and potentially appealing. This philosophy prioritizes the greater good over personal prejudices and preferences by calling for logical and objective governance. In a world where policy judgments are often tainted by personal agendas and emotional attachments, a more detached and unbiased decision-making process seems appealing. It promises to create a more egalitarian and just society based on logic and evidence rather than personal whims or emotional attachments. This method may yield more effective and efficient policies to solve the Policy decisions which can overcome subjective biases and personal agendas by emphasizing data and rationality. This unshakable dedication to objectivity and logic could lead to better outcomes for specific interest groups and society.

This method encourages policymakers to consider their potential effects and match them with public goals. Thus, evidence-based and logic-driven policymaking reduces subjective biases and ideological inclinations that can impede optimal outcomes, paving the way for a more equitable, efficient, and prosperous society.

Because of their deep roots in the human psyche, feelings and desires greatly influence our thoughts and actions. Unfortunately, this misperception may lead to unjust and discriminatory policies that prolong inequality and slow social progress. Thus, we must understand and challenge these biases to keep our collective awareness free of prejudice and our policies based on fairness, equality, and inclusivity. By overcoming these pressures on our thoughts and ideas, we may turn society into a more just, inclusive, and equitable place for all, regardless of background, identity, or circumstances. We may question the status quo and dismantle systemic barriers that perpetuate inequality and injustice by consciously rising above society conventions, cultural biases, and personal biases. Transcending encourages us to critically analyze our biases, prejudices, and privileges and actively engage in self-reflection and education to comprehend our experiences better.

Our daily lives are often influenced by short-term emotions and desires. These transitory sentiments confuse our judgment and impair our ability to understand our actions' long-term effects. We seem to wear metaphorical blinders that hinder us from seeing beyond our impulses' immediate fulfillment or satisfaction. This can be especially harmful when making life-changing decisions. Short-term emotions and desires might influence our logic and foresight by tempting us to indulge in unhealthy habits, make impulsive purchases, or act recklessly.

Thus, self-awareness and mindfulness are essential for We can navigate the complex world of decision-making and ensure that our decisions benefit present and future generations by adopting a more detached and analytical perspective. By separating ourselves from immediate emotions and impulses, we may move beyond short-term thinking and consider the long-term effects of our actions. This thorough and analytical approach helps us to examine the potential impact of our decisions on the social, economic, and environmental aspects of our world, allowing us to make choices that are actually in the best interests of our heirs.

When politicians, who are supposed to represent the public's interests and welfare, make decisions that prioritize personal gain or adhere rigidly to their own ideological beliefs rather than the public's needs and concerns, it can severely damage public trust in the government. Politicians have the power to restore public trust in politics by continually exhibiting neutrality and promoting the general good.

Emotions as a source of motivation: Human emotions, with their depth and intensity, can motivate us to make positive changes in our lives and the world. By purposefully concealing our emotions, we may lose the passion and commitment needed to solve complex life situations.

Innate human nature: In today's complex and ever-changing environment, it's difficult to expect or require that people entirely disconnect from their deepest feelings and desires. This becomes increasingly clearer when we consider complex and often divisive political matters. Artificially extending communication can lead to a sense of inauthenticity and a decreased ability to connect with voters.

To be an effective political leader, you must understand and appreciate the varied experiences and emotions of others. Leaders can promote inclusivity and unity by recognizing and empathizing with others' opinions and experiences. This knowledge helps them make decisions that consider the interests and aspirations of all citizens, not just a few. Leaders may also develop agreement and create more effective and sustainable policies by actively listening and engaging with other perspectives. We risk losing our ability to fully connect and empathize with the people we represent by consciously repressing our emotions.

The idea of an objective politician who makes decisions impartially has been debated and scrutinized. The potential consequences of such an ideal include that people with ulterior objectives could use this supposed neutrality to manipulate public opinion for their own gain. In today's complex and linked world, when political discourse is pushed by many interests and ideologies, a politician with perfect neutrality is intriguing and challenging. The idea of a leader who can ignore personal prejudices and make judgments based on evidence is enticing. It symbolizes political honesty and impartiality that is often lacking. It's important to remember that humans are subjective. Our upbringing and experiences shape our thoughts, beliefs, and values. A balance between reason and emotion is essential for a healthy, moral political system. This delicate balance is essential to building a fair, just, and equitable society for all. Recognizing the importance of reason and emotion can help us make judgments with care and consider human behavior's deep-rooted values and sentiments. This interaction between reason and emotion helps us understand difficult challenges and make logical, empathic, and compassionate decisions.

Different political philosophies may emphasize reason and emotion differently, which can lead to exciting and thought-provoking discussions. It is fascinating to see how different ideologies balance rationality and emotions in political decision-making and policymaking. Certain ideologies value logic and evidence-based arguments as the main drivers of political decision-making. They may think emotions should be controlled since they can impair judgment and cause rash decisions. However, other philosophies recognize that humans are not logical and see emotions as fundamental to political activity. These philosophies may claim that emotions reveal people's and communities' needs. Decision-making is a topic with many viewpoints. Many argue that rational decision-making should always be prioritized. This view holds that logical and objective decisions are more likely to succeed. They believe that by evaluating the pros and disadvantages, considering all the facts, and using critical thinking abilities, people can make good judgments.

Conversely, some believe emotions are crucial to decision-making. This concept holds that emotions motivate and drive change. They claim that reasonable conclusions may lack the passion and conviction needed to motivate action and growth.

The influence of emotions and personal prejudices on social media has grown in the digital era. Having reasonable debates regarding complex political topics has become difficult due to this phenomenon. Social media has changed political discourse by allowing people to rapidly share their views, opinions, and emotions with a large audience. However, this increased strength has downsides. The amplification of emotions on social media can cause polarization. Constantly being exposed to emotionally charged content makes it harder to approach political talks with an open mind and examine various ideas. People may retreat into echo chambers to bolster their beliefs and disregard dissent. This echo chamber effect reinforces preconceptions and hinders effective debate.

A well-informed public is essential for a healthy democracy. People's knowledge and awareness shape a democratic society's direction and success. Well-informed people can make better judgments, participate in democracy, and hold their elected authorities accountable.

Comprehensive education on the political process, critical thinking, and evidence-based decision-making can help foster informed political choices. We can enable people to make rational, non-emotional decisions by helping them comprehend these key factors.

We can strive to build a political system that is rational, logical, compassionate, and sympathetic by carefully evaluating all of these criteria. This political system would balance reason and emotion by carefully weaving and fluidly integrating both crucial parts in the relentless quest of society's mutual welfare and improvement.

In Stoicism, taking deliberate action and making decisions are crucial aspects of living a virtuous life. Here's an overview of how Stoicism approaches these concepts:

Prohairesis, Greek for "moral purpose" or "moral character," is the foundation of Stoic conduct. It includes the strongly held views, values, and principles that drive people's decisions and conduct. Stoics view prohairesis as Decision-making which is the cognitive process by which people choose among options.

Human agency is manifested when people use rational reasoning and moral discernment to make intentional choices. This process entails weighing a variety of considerations, considering the implications, and acting ethically. By making thoughtful and intentional decisions, people show they can rise beyond instinct and behave in accordance with their highest values. This includes the strongly held views, values, and principles that drive people's decisions and conduct.

Human agency is manifested when people use rational reasoning and moral discernment to make intentional choices. This process entails weighing a variety of considerations, considering the implications, and acting ethically. By making thoughtful and intentional decisions, people show they can rise beyond instinct and behave in accordance with their highest values.

Stoics, ancient philosophers noted for their wisdom and practical ideas, distinguished between things under our control and those without. Stoic philosophy centers on this dichotomy, which incorporates our thoughts, acts, and choices and external events, circumstances, and others' actions. Stoics believe that understanding this distinction is essential to inner serenity, tranquility, and fulfillment. Stoics believed that by focusing on their thoughts, attitudes, and behaviors, people may gain agency and autonomy over their life.

When taking purposeful action, we must remain focused on what we can control. By doing so, we can use reason and virtue to guide our actions. This purposeful approach helps us live with awareness and intention, allowing us to make decisions that reflect our values and goals. Virtue also ensures that our decisions are moral and ethical. This deliberate and thoughtful attitude empowers us to accept responsibility for our decisions, recognition that we can alter our fates via intentional action.

Stoics believe that as humans, we must always act in accordance with virtue. They claim that this duty is a fundamental obligation that we must fully and diligently fulfill. By following this Stoic principle, we can live a life of morality and inner peace, resulting in harmony with ourselves, others, and the world. To live virtuously, we must follow intelligence, courage, justice, and temperance. These four qualities guide our character and daily decisions. We show wisdom by analyzing the world and making educated decisions based on knowledge and experience. When taking purposeful action, we must carefully consider and assess the probable outcomes. This process demands us to carefully consider the possible results of our actions in light of our values. Doing so ensures that our decisions are cautious and deliberate. This intentional consideration helps us connect our behaviors with our core values and virtues.

Reason and Evidence: Ancient Greek philosophers the Stoics stressed the importance of using reason and facts to make decisions. Stoicism promotes rationality and logical thinking, encouraging people to analyze the evidence before making decisions. The Stoics' intellectual rigor and critical thinking are shown in their view that reason can help us understand and behave. Stoicism emphasizes reason and proof. To make an informed judgment in a difficult scenario, use a multi-step approach. This involves collecting a wide range of information from credible sources, carefully studying the situation from different angles, and objectively assessing the possibilities. This extensive approach helps people determine the best way to handle the situation.

The ancient Greek Stoics believed that emotions can cloud our judgment and lead to rash decisions. This perspective emphasizes the need to stay sensible and analytical, free from transient and irrational emotions. Stoics warn against letting emotions rule our choices and recommend a more calm and analytical approach to decision-making based on reason and evidence. They greatly promote impartial decision-making. They believe we must carefully analyze and acknowledge our emotions without letting them dominate our decisions. By retaining a balanced perspective, scientists believe we can make more reasoned and objective decisions without emotional bias. This method encourages people to step back, rationalize the issue, and assess the benefits and cons before making a choice. They stress the significance of reason and critical thinking and suggest that limiting emotions can help us make fact-based decisions.

Stoics, known for their philosophical insight, fully accept the profound idea that some aspects of our existence are beyond our control and must be accepted with equanimity. They strongly think that the universe's unpredictability often leads to events that don't match our hopes, forcing us to accept these truths. This method helps people make decisions without getting emotionally involved. Instead, they focus on thoroughly examining the information and using logic to choose the best option.

Political disagreement, antagonism, and rash decisions are common. This has prompted calls for Stoic leadership. Stoicism teaches us to control what we can, accept what we cannot, and live virtuously.

There are several reasons why Stoicism is particularly relevant to politics today:

Politics, a complex field, sometimes gets caught up in emotions, personal assaults, and strong ideological viewpoints. This regrettable tendency, which has occurred throughout history, hinders growth, healthy discourse, and common ground. When these elements dominate politics, they can overshadow reasonable discourse, compromise, and the collective Stoicism. Its core idea of rational thinking and objective decision-making is crucial to addressing today's complex political situations. Stoicism gives people the means to negotiate the political landscape with clarity and discernment.

Leaders often feel pressure to act quickly in the fast-paced world of leadership. Leaders must make quick, effective judgments, which can be daunting. However, this eagerness can lead to hasty and ill-considered decisions that can have negative consequences. Leaders may act without considering the ramifications in a fast-changing circumstance. Impulsive behavior can result from fear of indecision or a desire to dominate the situation. Leaders must reject these influences and prioritize thoughtful deliberation. Stoicism teaches us to pause, contemplate, and weigh all choices before acting. Founded on the teachings of Epictetus, Seneca, and Marcus Aurelius, this fundamental concept guides our daily lives and emphasizes the significance of slow, thoughtful and deliberate decision-making.

Political fragmentation is one of the biggest obstacles to problem-solving in today's complicated and linked society. Unfortunately, this polarizing phenomenon sometimes hinders leaders' collaboration and cooperation, which is essential for solving society's many challenges. Political conflict at the local, national, and international levels hinders development and leaders' efforts to address critical challenges. Stoicism encourages cooperation, fairness, and a strong commitment to the common good. These concepts give Stoicism a great framework for bridging gaps and uniting various people. The Stoic principle of cooperation encourages people to work together toward common goals. This collaborative approach fosters camaraderie and mutual support and allows varied perspectives and talents to be pooled, resulting in more imaginative and successful solutions. Stoicism values cooperation because it understands the power of collective efforts, creating a society that thrives on collaboration rather than competition.

With its complex power dynamics, continuous media scrutiny, and high-stakes decision-making, politics is one of the most stressful and challenging environments. Stoicism offers many tools and techniques to manage stress, stay calm under pressure, and most importantly, stay focused on what matters most in life. Stoicism's deep knowledge and practical insights help people navigate life's complexity and find peace in the modern world. Stoic philosophers like Epictetus, Marcus Aurelius, and Seneca offer a wealth of wisdom that helps people overcome adversity.

Stoicism places a profound emphasis on the utmost significance of consistently and unwaveringly acting in accordance with virtue and integrity. This philosophical doctrine continues to resonate with individuals across various cultures and generations. It encourages individuals to cultivate a moral compass that guides their actions and decisions in a manner that is aligned with the principles of virtue and integrity. In today's complex and ever-changing world, it has become increasingly crucial to prioritize the task of building trust and restoring faith in our political institutions. This imperative cannot be overstated, as the very foundation of our democratic society relies on the belief that our elected officials and governing bodies are acting in the best interest of the people they serve.

Here are some examples of historical figures who embodied Stoic principles in their leadership.

Marcus Aurelius

From 161 to 180 AD, the Roman emperor was a major character in Roman history. He faced many problems and made crucial decisions that built the empire. Despite political challenges, his rule was successful and difficult. He felt that virtue, reason, and duty were the foundation for a meaningful and fulfilling life. He passionately lived these ideals and used his influence to improve the lives of those he helped. He worked relentlessly to improve his people's well-being and quality of life by using his authority and resources. He left no stone unturned in his pursuit of growth and prosperity. His passion for community improvement and adherence to his ideas demonstrate true leadership and selflessness.

George Washington

George Washington, the America's founding father, shaped history. From 1789 until 1797, he was the first president of the United States, shaping the country's politics with his passion and vision. Washington guided the promising nation through its early years, creating vital precedents and laying the groundwork for a strong and successful nation. He led the Continental Army during the Revolutionary War, demonstrating his tactical and strategic skills. In addition to his military successes, Washington carefully polished his leadership style, drawing from Stoicism's timeless precepts.

He believed reason was essential in all aspects of life, personal and social. He preached moderation, believing that a careful balance in all undertakings yielded the best results. The extremes of any spectrum are dangerous, hence he strongly advised against them.

Nelson Mandela

As South Africa's president from 1994 to 1999, anti-apartheid leader Nelson Mandela shaped its history. He inspired millions of people worldwide with his unrelenting devotion to justice and equality. Mandela was admired worldwide for his persistent efforts to overthrow apartheid and construct a democratic society based on inclusivity and human rights.

Drew was inspired by Stoicism, which emphasizes inner fortitude and resilience, throughout his administration in his unrelenting pursuit of personal freedom and emancipation from societal limitations.

He believed in overcoming adversity with courage and resilience. He spent his life working to create a fair and equitable society where everyone has equal opportunity and is respected and honored.

Winston Churchill

The World War II British Prime Minister was a brilliant leader who changed history. He led the nation through one of its most difficult moments with his unflinching determination, skillful leadership, and unmatched resilience. He will always be remembered for his daring, tenacity, and steadfast commitment to freedom. He is revered for his tenacity, resilience, and unrelenting perseverance in the face of life's obstacles.

Despite the worst conditions, this exceptional person maintained his stoic attitude throughout the conflict. It is amazing how he kept his composure and gave the British people hope amid the worst days of the war. His persistent resolve and attitude inspired many to persevere and overcome adversity. His exceptional character and leadership allowed him to remain calm and steadfast under such chaos, leaving an unforgettable impression on the British people.

Mahatma Gandhi

Gandhi was a leading figure in India's freedom movement and a symbol of nonviolence. He exemplified the eternal stoic principles of self-control, discipline, and inner tranquility, which have been cherished and practiced throughout history. By following these principles, he showed a deep knowledge of the significance of controlling emotions, ideas, and actions, enabling handling life's obstacles with grace. Self-control allowed him to resist instant gratification, and his message of peace, justice, and equality has inspired millions worldwide.

Dalai Lama

The Tibetan spiritual leader is esteemed and influential, providing his followers with insight and guidance. With roots in ancient traditions and teachings, this person exhibits the stoic virtues of compassion, knowledge, and inner calm, which are praiseworthy and guide others. They show incredible empathy and kindness because they comprehend the human predicament. A calm and cool approach to life's issues and smart guidance show in his actions and words.

He is a great person who has inspired people worldwide with his powerful and thought-provoking message of tolerance and acceptance. He has inspired compassion and empathy in many people by his words and acts. He inspires hope in a divided society with his persistent dedication to harmony and acceptance.

History is full of political leaders who have shown stoicism and integrity. These extraordinary people have inspired future generations with their acts and values. Their unrelenting devotion to justice, fairness, and ethics has earned them a position among great leaders. Their stories demonstrate the political potency of stoicism and integrity. Many people throughout history have shown that it is possible and admirable to live a life of integrity and purpose, even in the most difficult circumstances. These amazing people have shown us that the human spirit can overcome adversity and embrace a greater calling, encouraging us to strive for greatness. These exceptional people have exhibited steadfast persistence, resilience, and commitment to their values and ideas over seemingly insurmountable difficulties. They showed that one's character and integrity can survive the hardest situations. Their stories demonstrate the strength of the human spirit and our boundless potential. From historical giants who changed the world to everyday heroes whose generosity and altruism have impacted others, these exceptional people who have left an everlasting imprint on history inspire others from all walks of life. Their incredible stories and achievements inspire us to improve and evolve. Their lives model knowledge, courage, justice, and temperance, which we should all strive for. Their wisdom, gained from life experiences and deep contemplation, helps us make good judgments and find the truth in confusion. They overcame difficulties and daunting trials, inspiring us to face our anxieties and embrace the unknown with tenacity.

Chapter 12

Leading at Home with a Stoic Heart

"The only true wealth is the wealth of your relationships."

Lao Tzu

*B*eing a leader isn't just about boardrooms and big decisions. The most important leadership role we often play is right in our own home, guiding our families with love, patience, and wisdom. But let's be honest, families can be messy, full of tantrums, meltdowns, and the occasional flying spaghetti monster (or its equivalent). So how can we stay calm, collected, and inspiring in the face of domestic chaos? That's where Stoicism comes in.

Let's face it, families are like a box of assorted LEGOs: colorful, messy, and sometimes missing an important piece (where did that other sock go?). Now, you might be thinking, "Stoicism? Isn't that all about logic and reason? What does that have to do with tantrums and bedtime battles?"

Leading at home with a Stoic heart means being a good leader in your family by following some important principles. Let's talk about how you can do this.

1. Making Good Choices:

- What is important to you? Think about your values and what matters most to you.
- Decide carefully: Use your mind to make good choices that match your values.

2. Controlling What You Can:

- Think about what you can control: There are things you can change and things you can't. Focus on what you can change.
- Stay calm: Don't let things you can't change bother you. Stay calm and think about what you can do.

3. Being a Good Example:

- Show how to be good: Act in a way that shows others how to be kind and fair.
- Be honest: Always tell the truth. This helps people trust you.

4. Understanding Others:

- Listen and understand: Pay attention when others talk and try to understand how they feel.
- Care about them: Show that you care about the people in your family. Understand their feelings.

5. Handling Tough Times:

- Stay strong: When things are hard, be strong. Don't give up easily.
- Find solutions: Think about how to solve problems instead of just worrying about them.

6. Keeping Calm:

- Stay calm in tough moments: When things get tough, try to stay calm. It helps you make better decisions.
- Don't let feelings take over: Feelings are okay, but don't let them control everything. Think with a clear mind.

7. Working Together:

- Teamwork is important: Help each other in the family. Teamwork makes everything easier.
- Solve problems together: When there's a problem, work together to find a solution.

8. Showing Love and Care:

- Be loving: Show your family that you care about them. Small acts of kindness show love and make a big difference.
- Appreciate each other: Say thank you and show that you appreciate what others do.

9. Learning from Stoic Leaders:

- Look at leaders from history: People like Marcus Aurelius and Nelson Mandela were great leaders. Learn from them.
- Use Stoic ideas: Stoicism teaches useful ideas. Think about how Stoic principles can help you lead at home.

10. Growing Together:

- Learn and grow: Keep learning new things. Growing together makes your family stronger.
- Make mistakes and learn: It's okay to make mistakes. Learn from them and become better.

Stoicism isn't about turning your home into a Roman temple. It's about cultivating a mindset that helps you direct life's ups and downs with grace and strength. Here are a few Stoic principles that can make you a rockstar leader (or at least a more chilled-out one) in your own household:

1. Focus on what you can control: Let's face it, you can't control your child's love for finger painting on the walls, or your teenager's questionable music taste. But you can control your reaction. Instead of losing your cool, take a deep breath, remember the "dichotomy of control," and focus on what you can do – like offering alternative art supplies, or maybe investing in some noise-canceling headphones.

2. Embrace the present moment: Stop dwelling on past meltdowns or worrying about future messes. Be present with your family, savor the silly moments, and appreciate the quiet ones. Remember, even the most chaotic phases pass, and you'll miss these days when they're gone. Think of yourself as a time-traveling chef, savoring the ingredients of the present to create a delicious family recipe.

3. Practice mindfulness: Dishes piling up? Toddler screaming? Take a minute to pause and observe your emotions without judgment. Are you feeling overwhelmed? Frustrated? Angry? Acknowledge it, then let it go. Like a cloud passing across the

sky, your emotions are temporary. Mindfulness helps you to be the calm in the storm, the stable lighthouse in a sea of tantrums.

4. Let go of perfectionism: Your house doesn't have to be Instagram-worthy, and your kids don't need to be mini-Einsteins. Accept that chaos is part of life, and even celebrate it sometimes! A perfectly picked-up playroom is just a missed opportunity for blanket forts and pillow fights. Remember, the best memories are often made in the messiest moments.

5. Lead with virtue: Be the role model you want your family to see. Show them kindness, even when they're acting like little monsters. Show them patience, even when they're testing your limits. Show them courage, even when you're facing your own fears. By embodying Stoic virtues, you'll inspire them to do the same, creating a home filled with understanding, resilience, and maybe even a little less finger painting on the walls.

Think of your family as the crew on your life-ship, sailing through the sometimes-stormy seas of everyday life. Stoicism helps you become a captain who pilots calmly, keeping everyone feeling safe and secure. Here's how:

Remember those mornings when choosing breakfast feels like an epic battle? Stoic principles like focusing on the "dichotomy of control" come in handy. You can't control whether the kids want pancakes or cereal, but you can control how you present the options. Instead of getting stressed, offer choices calmly, knowing you can't please everyone all the time. This teaches your family to think critically and make their own choices, fostering independence and confidence.

Stoicism teaches you not to be a puppet on the strings of your emotions. So, when the dog throws up on the rug, instead of going ballistic, you can take a deep breath, assess the situation calmly, and delegate tasks with humor. This shows your family that even messy mishaps can be handled with grace, and they learn to approach challenges with a similar level head.

Remember how Stoics emphasize virtue and logic? This translates into a home where everyone feels respected and heard. Practice active listening, understand different perspectives, and offer support instead of judgment. This creates a safe space where everyone feels comfortable expressing themselves, knowing they'll be met with love and understanding. Imagine a home where siblings can confide in each other, and parents are open to hearing even the most awkward teenage questions. That's the power of Stoic communication.

Remember, your family observes you. So, when you practice Stoic principles, they're subtly learning by watching. Be the one who apologizes when you're wrong, who forgives freely, and who shows gratitude for even the smallest acts of kindness. These actions become the norm, creating a home where everyone feels valued and responsible for contributing to the overall well-being.

Embracing the Imperfect Joy: Stoicism doesn't mean living in a sterile museum. It's about embracing the beautiful chaos of life. So, laugh with your kids when they build a precarious Lego tower that inevitably crashes. Celebrate silly mistakes and remind everyone that perfection is overrated. This creates a home filled with genuine laughter, where everyone feels comfortable being their authentic selves, Legos and all.

Families are like superheroes after a battle royale: bruised, exhausted, and maybe missing a sock or two. But amidst the spilled juice boxes and homework meltdowns, a Stoic heart can be your secret superpower. It's not about turning into Captain Logic or raising mini philosophers, but about creating a home that feels like a fortress of calm, even when the world outside is throwing everything at you.

Decisions are made with a clear head, not a temper tantrum. Instead of yelling "clean your room!", you calmly guide your mini heroes, focusing on what they can control (like choosing their clothes) and teaching them responsibility. This avoids power struggles and creates a team atmosphere.

Honest talk, not mind-reading, is your superpower. Listen with open ears, even when your teenager is speaking in grunts and sighs. Acknowledge their feelings, offer support, and speak your truth with kindness. This builds trust and promotes genuine connections, even when things get messy.

Fairness is your motto. Whether it's bedtime routines or chores, everyone gets treated with respect, regardless of age or size. Set clear expectations, explain the "whys" behind the rules, and enforce them consistently. This creates a sense of security and teaches everyone the value of justice and responsibility.

Even when the laundry monster attacks and the kitchen resembles a battlefield, remember to celebrate the small victories. Say "thank you" for the messy hugs, the silly jokes, and even the attempts to help (even if they involve Legos and glitter). This boosts everyone's mood and reminds you that even chaos can be beautiful.

Remember, perfectionism is the enemy. Stoicism teaches you to embrace the mess and focus on what you can control. So, instead of freaking out over a spilled smoothie, take a breath, laugh it off, and work together to clean it up. This teaches everyone that mistakes are part of life and resilience is key.

Show your family how to be Stoic superheroes. Apologize when you're wrong, forgive freely, and handle stress with grace. They'll learn by watching you, and soon, you'll have a whole team of mini-Stoics navigating life's challenges with a calm mind and a kind heart.

Scenario 1:

Bedtime Battleground

Non-Stoic Leader: Loses their cool, yells about bedtime routine. Feels frustrated and powerless.

Stoic Leader: Takes a deep breath, calmly explains the importance of sleep. Offers a bedtime story, creating a positive association. Feels in control and connected.

Scenario 2:

Teenager's Meltdown

Non-Stoic Leader: Reacts angrily, blames teenager, escalates the situation. Feels overwhelmed and hurt.

Stoic Leader: Listens actively, acknowledges their feelings. Offers support and space, avoids judgment. Feels calm and understanding, fosters trust.

Scenario 3:

Lost Sock Mystery

Non-Stoic Leader: Starts accusing, blames kids, turns into a sock detective. Feels stressed and angry.

Stoic Leader: Focuses on what they can control – searching calmly, offering suggestions. Reminds everyone it's just a sock. Feels neutral and resourceful, avoids unnecessary tension.

Scenario 4:

Chores Chaos

Non-Stoic Leader: Interferes, yells at kids for not doing things right. Feels frustrated and overworked.

Stoic Leader: Sets clear expectations, empowers kids to choose their tasks. Offers guidance but avoids hovering. Feels trusting and supportive, encourages responsibility.

Scenario 5:

Dinner Disaster

Non-Stoic Leader: Gets angry at burnt pizza, blames everyone, takes it personally. Feels upset and defeated.

Stoic Leader: Laughs it off, reminds everyone it's just food. Works together to fix the situation, improvises a new meal. Feels adaptable and positive, turns a mishap into a bonding experience.

Scenario 6:

Decision Deadline

Non-Stoic Leader: Gets stressed, makes impulsive choices based on fear. Feels anxious and uncertain.

Stoic Leader: Weighs options rationally, considers everyone's needs. Make a clear decision based on logic and fairness. Feels confident and responsible, inspires trust in the family.

Scenario 7:

Unexpected Expense

Non-Stoic Leader: Panics, blames external factors, feels like a victim.

Stoic Leader: Remains calm evaluates the situation objectively. Adjusts the budget, seeks solutions without blaming. Feels resourceful and resilient, avoids helplessness.

Scenario 8:

Family Time Dilemma

Non-Stoic Leader: Gets frustrated by everyone's different preferences, forces a shared activity. Feels resentful and disconnected.

Stoic Leader: Listens to everyone's needs, encourages open communication. Finds a compromise activity everyone can enjoy. Feels connected and understanding, fosters a sense of belonging.

In our homes, where families come together like a mix quilt of fathers, mothers, sisters, brothers, and all kinds of relatives, creating a sense of safety and comfort is vital.

In leading at home with a Stoic heart, we craft not just a dwelling but a haven where every family member finds solace, strength, and love. Stoicism becomes the gentle breeze that guides us through the ups and downs, creating a home where hearts are at peace and souls are nourished by the wisdom of the Stoic way.

Families come in all shapes and sizes, with different roles and relationships. Stoicism is like the thread that weaves through, creating a strong and united fabric of love and understanding.

Whether you're a grandparent, aunt, uncle, cousin, or any kind of kin, Stoicism reminds us that each person in the family is important. Every heart contributes to the melody of home.

Stoicism teaches us to make our home a sanctuary—a place where everyone feels safe, accepted, and loved. It's a shelter from life's storms, where you can be yourself.

Stoicism provides a comforting philosophy, emphasizing resilience, virtue, and reason. These principles act as pillars, supporting the emotional well-being of every family member.

Just as leaders in the world inspire through Stoic principles, parents and elders can lead with a Stoic heart at home. Demonstrating strength, wisdom, and kindness sets the tone.

Children and other family members often learn by watching. When leaders showcase Stoic values in their actions, it becomes a natural part of the family culture.

Stoicism encourages attentive listening. Taking the time to understand each other fosters open communication. A Stoic home is one where everyone's voice is heard.

Stoicism doesn't dismiss emotions but encourages expressing them honestly. Sharing feelings creates an environment of trust and understanding.

When challenges arise, a Stoic family stands together. Supporting each other through difficulties, celebrating victories, and being a rock for one another builds a resilient family bond.

Stoicism teaches courage in the face of adversity. Families can tackle challenges with strength, knowing they have each other's backs.

Stoicism aligns with many universal values—virtue, kindness, resilience. Identifying and embracing shared family values creates a common ground for everyone.

Establishing family traditions based on Stoic principles can be a source of joy and connection. These traditions strengthen the family's identity.

Stoicism emphasizes understanding and respecting each person's uniqueness. In a Stoic home, differences are not just tolerated but celebrated.

Individuals within the family can grow together while pursuing their own paths. Stoicism encourages personal development within the context of a supportive family.

Stoicism encourages the practice of gratitude. A Stoic home is one where family members appreciate the good in each other and count their blessings.

Love is at the core of Stoic teachings. Expressing love through actions, words, and gestures strengthens the family bond.

Incorporating Stoic wisdom into family discussions and teachings helps instill valuable life lessons.

Stoic homes create memories based on virtue, resilience, and compassion. These memories become a legacy passed down through generations.

Stoicism is not a destination but a journey. Families grow together, learning from Stoic principles and applying them to daily life.

Just as Stoicism is a gift to the world; it becomes a cherished gift within the walls of a Stoic home. It shapes character, nurtures relationships, and creates a haven of warmth and understanding.

Nurturing Family Bonds with Stoic Wisdom

The Stormy Argument

Setting: Your family is caught in a heated argument. Emotions are running high, and words are sharp.

Stoic Approach: Instead of reacting impulsively, take a moment to breathe. Apply Stoic principles of rationality and logic to understand different perspectives. Respond calmly, fostering a more thoughtful conversation and preventing unnecessary hurt.

Tough Parenting Decision

Setting: As a parent, you face a difficult decision regarding your child's future. The choices seem overwhelming, and emotions are clouding your judgment.

Stoic Approach: Stoicism guides you to separate emotions from decisions. Analyze the situation objectively, weighing the pros and cons. By making a reasoned choice, you ensure that the decision is in the best interest of your child and the family as a whole.

Sibling Rivalry

Setting: Your children are in the midst of a typical sibling fight. Tensions are escalating, and it's challenging to keep the peace.

Stoic Approach: Rather than getting emotionally involved, practice Stoic empathy. Understand the underlying issues, encourage open communication, and guide your children in resolving conflicts peacefully. Stoicism teaches the value of harmony and cooperation.

Dealing with Loss

Setting: Your family is grieving the loss of a beloved pet. Emotions are raw, and everyone copes differently.

Stoic Approach: Stoicism helps you acknowledge and express emotions honestly. Support each family member through the grieving process with compassion and understanding. Stoic principles of resilience and acceptance become pillars during challenging times.

Balancing Work and Family

Setting: The demands of work are making it challenging to spend quality time with your family. Guilt and stress are affecting your well-being.

Stoic Approach: Stoicism encourages prioritizing what you can control. Focus on the quality of time spent with family rather than quantity. By applying Stoic principles of acceptance and finding balance, you can navigate work pressures without compromising family connections.

Extended Family Dynamics

Setting: Different family members have varying opinions on a significant family event. Disagreements are creating tension.

Stoic Approach: Apply Stoic principles of respect and understanding. Encourage open dialogue, allowing each family member to express their views. By fostering a sense of inclusivity and unity, Stoicism contributes to a more harmonious extended family dynamic.

Financial Challenges

Setting: Your family is facing financial difficulties, leading to stress and uncertainty about the future.

Stoic Approach: Stoicism guides you to focus on what you can control—budgeting, planning, and supporting each other emotionally. By applying Stoic principles of resilience and practicality, you can navigate financial challenges with a clear and rational mindset.

Celebrating Achievements

Setting: A family member has achieved a significant milestone, and you want to celebrate together.

Stoic Approach: Stoicism emphasizes gratitude and appreciation. Celebrate achievements with genuine joy, expressing love and support. Stoic principles of joy in others' successes contribute to a positive and uplifting family environment.

In every scenario, Stoicism serves as a guiding light, promoting logical and rational actions. By encouraging a home grounded in rationality, families can build deeper connections, make thoughtful decisions, and create an atmosphere of safety and comfort. Leading by example with a Stoic heart contributes to the well-being and harmony of the entire family, irrespective of its diverse composition.

Building a home with Stoic bricks isn't about being a robot parent. It's about creating a space where everyone can be their authentic selves, where logic and love go hand-in-hand, and where even the most tangled Lego creations can be admired, not dreaded. It's about creating a haven where everyone feels safe, respected, and empowered. By practicing its principles, you become the leader who faces life's storms with a calm hand, keeping your family safe in the harbor of your love.

Conclusion

*A*lthough there are several leadership styles that can be applied to different situations, there are many commonalities that underpin all good leadership. Successful leadership requires cultivating these common threads to inspire and drive teams toward shared goals and objectives.

Vision and Direction: Leaders inspire people and motivate them to work toward a common goal through this vision. They can explain complex concepts to their team, stakeholders, or the larger community. One of these outstanding people's greatest gifts is encouraging their followers to greatness. Due to their great leadership skills, they can build a clear and captivating image of what can be done. They generate a tremendous sense of shared purpose that connects everyone towards a single goal by expertly developing a vision that resonates with their audience. The fact that they can delve into their followers' deepest dreams and desires and motivate them to achieve greatness is a testimonial to their leadership skills. Leaders leave a lasting impression on those they touch by their persistent commitment to uplifting and motivating others.

Integrity and Trust: Trust is vital for every successful leadership relationship. It is essential and cannot be ignored. Without trust, a leadership relationship is like a fragile building that could collapse at any time. Effective leaders build trust with their followers by consistently demonstrating integrity, honesty, and ethical standards. Leaders must build trust to create a good and productive workplace. Leaders inspire confidence in their followers by acting with integrity, demonstrating their capacity to make good decisions and serve the team or company. Leaders who communicate honestly and transparently foster an environment of openness and authenticity, which encourages teamwork and dialogue. They are notable for their consistency in words and behavior. Their sincerity and reliability are shown by their extraordinary ability to match words with actions. This consistency is embedded in their character and shows through in every part of their lives. Their decision-making accountability is commendable. They accept responsibility for their decisions, whether they succeed or fail.

Communication and Relationship Building: Any organization or team needs leaders to guide and inspire their members. Communicating vision, plans, and expectations to team members is a hallmark of great leaders. Leadership relies on good communication. It helps leaders clearly communicate their ideas, plans, and goals to ensure everyone is on the same page and working toward a common goal. Leaders inspire their teams to excel by sharing their vision. Leaders with good communication skills stand out for their active listening skills. They go the extra mile to understand and value their followers' opinions. Active listening fosters a safe, inclusive environment that welcomes open discourse. This safe zone allows people to share their opinions without condemnation freely. They also work to build respectful, understanding connections with their followers. They value genuine connections and aim to build community with their audience. Through constant participation and genuine interest in their followers' lives, they build a link beyond social media.

Decision-Making and Problem-Solving: Effective leaders who can guide and inspire others to success make decisions by analyzing evidence, using logic, and carefully considering the potential consequences of their choices. They are brave while consulting others and seeking diverse opinions. People with good analytical and problem-solving skills can critically analyze difficult circumstances and find effective answers. Their data analysis and pattern recognition skills help them solve complex issues and provide new solutions. These people are also adept at adapting to new situations, showing their flexibility and agility in dynamic surroundings.

Empowerment and Delegation: Effective leaders know they can't do everything alone. They need this knowledge to lead and manage a team or organization. These leaders can leverage their team's power and knowledge by accepting their limitations and embracing collaboration, resulting in better success and goal achievement. By giving their team members important tasks, they show their confidence in them and let them shine. Delegation reduces the leader's workload and gives followers a sense of pride and success. Along with delegating, great leaders know that followers need resources. They know their team members may struggle to succeed without the right tools and assistance. They work to provide their followers access to resources. Additionally, great leaders know that teamwork drives invention.

Learning and Development: Effective leaders believe continuous learning is crucial to leadership and seek opportunities to extend their perspectives and improve their skills. These leaders are insatiably curious and hungry for new ideas to improve their leadership skills. They know the world is ever-changing, therefore they must adapt to stay ahead. They actively promote their team members' professional development since they prioritize knowledge acquisition and advancement. They give their staff workshops, seminars, and training programs to improve their skills and stay ahead in their fields. This drive to personal and professional improvement improves team members' skills and the organization's performance and creativity. Their willingness to receive feedback is remarkable.

Motivation and Inspiration: Effective leaders have the ability to inspire and motivate others. Positive and motivating work environments provide these leaders' teams a sense of purpose and energy that drives them ahead. They motivate their followers to believe in their potential and capabilities, creating a supportive and empowering environment. They inspire their followers to reach for the stars and discover their boundless potential via genuine appreciation and joy. The organization fosters creativity, innovation, and devotion in its employees by creating a good and supportive work environment.

Self-Awareness and Self-Discipline: Effective leaders have great self-awareness and know their strengths and flaws. They believe self-improvement is lifelong and strive to develop their leadership skills. This perspective drives them to seek out growth and development through self-reflection, feedback, and learning situations. These leaders know that investing in their own growth improves their leadership and inspires and empowers others to succeed. Thus, their commitment to self-improvement generates a healthy, innovative, and growing organizational culture. and Self-discipline and emotional and behavioral management set exceptional people distinct. Their self-control and reaction control are admirable. Unwavering self-discipline helps leaders stay focused and make progress toward their goals. Additionally, their emotional intelligence and self-awareness help individuals comprehend and control their emotions. Their capacity to lead by example is outstanding.

Service and Contribution: Effective leaders who can inspire and lead their teams to success believe in their job as humble servants who care about others. These extraordinary leaders foster trust, collaboration, and empowerment by knowing that leadership is about selflessly supporting and uplifting people they lead. They understand that their primary responsibility is to serve their team members, foster their development, and meet their needs. They are driven by a deep desire to make a lasting positive impact on the world and leave things better than they found them. They stand out for their unwavering dedication to their followers' achievement. They always go above and above to help their team or organization. As they put their followers' needs and goals first, their dedication to their growth and happiness is encouraging. They are a role model for their great leadership and dedication to others' well-being.

Seek continuous improvement: Stoicism emphasizes lifelong learning and personal progress. This ancient Greek and Roman philosophical school supports lifelong learning, intellectual growth, and personal development. By following Stoic ideals, leaders who are dedicated to personal growth and development show an insatiable desire to learn and evolve. Their relentless pursuit of self-improvement improves their leadership skills and inspires others to do the same. Stoic leaders are perpetual learners who seek new challenges and opportunities to grow.

Stoic leaders strive to be rational, objective, and resilient, and their leadership tactics often revolve around these core principles. Here are some key tactics employed by stoic leaders:

Focus on what you can control: Stoicism inspires the human spirit. Stoicism teaches us that true happiness and well-being may be attained by focusing on what we can control rather than the unpredictable and frequently uncontrollable external situations. In a world full of distractions and obstacles, Stoicism reminds us to change our viewpoint and adopt a mindset that helps us handle life's challenges with grace and resilience. By focusing on what we can control, we free ourselves from anxiety and frustration caused by external factors. Stoic leaders, noted for their uncompromising adherence to the philosophy, apply this key concept in their daily lives. They deliberately focus on their actions, decisions, and responses rather than extraneous circumstances that may detract from their aims. By retaining this consistent perspective, these leaders can handle the complexities of their roles with calm and serenity, allowing them to make good decisions and lead their people with purpose.

Practice self-awareness and reflection: Stoic leaders, known for their strong commitment to self-improvement, engage in a consistent and profound practice of introspection. This introspective process involves a deep exploration of their inner world, meticulously examining their thoughts, emotions, and actions. By delving into the depths of their being, these leaders gain invaluable insights into their own strengths and weaknesses, enabling them to identify areas for growth and development. Through this ongoing process of self-reflection, stoic leaders

261

continuously refine their character and enhance their leadership abilities, ultimately becoming more effective and impactful in their roles. One of the remarkable aspects of self-awareness is its ability to empower individuals to effectively manage their own reactions and steer clear of making impulsive decisions. By cultivating a deep understanding of their own thoughts, emotions, and behaviors, individuals become equipped with the invaluable skill of introspection. This heightened level of self-awareness enables them to navigate through life's challenges with a sense of clarity and composure, as they are able to recognize and regulate their own responses.

Manage emotions effectively: Stoicism emphasizes the importance of reason above emotion in daily life. This philosophical system promotes a logical worldview to help people navigate life with wisdom and peace. Stoic leaders try to regulate their emotions and stay calm in different situations. These leaders can inspire others by being firm in the face of hardship and maintaining stability and resilience through emotional self-regulation. People can make educated decisions that match their long-term aims and values by carefully considering their options and their potential repercussions. When people can separate themselves from transient emotions and use logic, they are less likely to be influenced by external forces.

Lead by example: Stoic leaders believe that effective leadership requires leading by example, continually demonstrating the ideals and behaviors they expect from their people. They inspire and motivate their team by embracing these ideas, which underpin their leadership style. This consistent dedication to setting a great example promotes integrity, responsibility, trust, and respect in the team, boosting productivity and success. They always walk the walk, showing unflinching integrity, honesty, and excellent ethics that inspires others who witness them. This behavior and attitude sets a high bar for others, inspiring them to constantly strive and achieve greatness in all parts of their lives.

Prioritize stoic exercises: Stoic leaders, famed for their calmness and resilience, use a variety of stoic exercises to improve themselves. These centuries-old activities include writing, meditation, and negative visualization. Stoic leaders develop self-awareness and emotional stability by incorporating these practices into their daily routines, helping them to handle adversities with grace and wisdom. Journaling lets them reflect on their thoughts. Regularly practicing these activities can help people develop self-awareness and comprehend their thoughts, feelings, and actions. Actively exploring and reflecting on one's inner landscape can increase self-awareness and empower one to make better daily decisions. These activities also help people manage their emotions.

People can learn to detect and manage their emotions for good by using numerous methods. This makes difficult situations easier and boosts emotional resilience and well-being.

Develop a clear vision and communicate effectively: Stoic leaders, recognized for their calmness and resilience, have a clear vision for the future that guides their teams. They inspire and drive their team with their outstanding ability to explain this vision, giving them purpose and direction. Leaders that effectively communicate their vision unite their teams behind a common goal. Their clarity of purpose and ability to communicate inspires confidence and trust in their team members and motivates them to succeed, propelling the firm forward. Effective communication is the foundation for an engaged and high-performing team, therefore leaders must prioritize it.

In conclusion, Stoicism stresses communication and delegation along with its core principles. Communicating their goal and giving their staff the necessary tools can motivate employees. Leadership may provide teams purpose and direction by communicating their vision. Stoicism, when respected, may be seamlessly integrated into various leadership styles with consistent practice and self-discipline.

Stoicism promotes reason, ethics, and resilience, making it a great leadership framework. Ancient Greek stoicism offers great leadership ideas today. Stoicism advises sensible leaders. The complete embrace of these ideals can build a powerful and satisfying leadership style that drives success. Unwavering dedication to these principles helps leaders retain inner serenity, which positively impacts their teams and fosters growth, innovation, and achievement.

About the Author

F. Zeth Lent has decades of life experience that primarily focuses on the success and well-being of people. Throughout both his professional and personal life, he has discovered the pivotal role of the advocate. Rooted in a traditional value system that extends back millennia to biblical and Roman Empire thought. He has championed the causes and dreams of countless individuals, embodying the spirit of support and empowerment.

A masterful storyteller, F. Zeth Lent utilizes his wealth of life experiences to craft narratives that inspire, motivate, and resonate with readers from all walks of life. Drawing from a diverse array of influences, his works transcend genres, whisking readers away on thought-provoking journeys that explore the complexities of the human condition. From insightful guides that offer practical wisdom to explorations of historical and philosophical concepts, F. Zeth Lent's books are imbued with the wisdom of a life dedicated to the advocacy of others, leaving an enduring mark on the literary landscape.